ELIZABETH AUDU

THE NARROW
GATE

Strait is the path that leads to eternal life

ELIZABETH AUDU

THE NARROW GATE

Strait is the path that leads to eternal life

MEREO
Cirencester

Mereo Books

1A The Wool Market Dyer Street Cirencester Gloucestershire GL7 2PR
An imprint of Memoirs Publishing www.mereobooks.com

The Narrow Gate: 978-1-86151-718-0

First published in Great Britain in 2016
by Mereo Books, an imprint of Memoirs Publishing

Copyright ©2016

Elizabeth Audu has asserted her right under the Copyright Designs and Patents
Act 1988 to be identified as the author of this work.

Unless otherwise indicated, Bible quotations are taken from
the King James Version of the Holy Bible.

This book is a work of fiction and except in the case of historical fact any
resemblance to actual persons living or dead is purely coincidental.

A CIP catalogue record for this book is available from the British Library.

This book is sold subject to the condition that it shall not by way of trade or
otherwise be lent, resold, hired out or otherwise circulated without the publisher's
prior consent in any form of binding or cover, other than that in which it is
published and without a similar condition, including this condition being imposed
on the subsequent purchaser.

The address for Memoirs Publishing Group Limited can be found at
www.memoirspublishing.com

The Memoirs Publishing Group Ltd Reg. No. 7834348

The Memoirs Publishing Group supports both The Forest Stewardship Council®
(FSC®) and the PEFC® leading international forest-certification organisations. Our
books carrying both the FSC label and the PEFC® and are printed on FSC®-certified
paper. FSC® is the only forest-certification scheme supported by the leading
environmental organisations including Greenpeace. Our paper procurement policy
can be found at www.memoirspublishing.com/environment

Typeset in 12/18pt Century Schoolbook
by Wiltshire Associates Publisher Services Ltd. Printed and bound in Great Britain
by Printondemand-Worldwide, Peterborough PE2 6XD

CONTENTS

Dedication
Acknowledgements
About the Author
Introduction

Chapter 1	God's Commandment	P.1
Chapter 2	Love	P.22
Chapter 3	Fasting and Prayers	P.47
Chapter 4	Forgiveness	P.61
Chapter 5	Subdue the Flesh	P.66
Chapter 6	Encouragement	P.75
Chapter 7	Slothfulness	P.85
Chapter 8	Preparedness	P.102
Chapter 9	The Word	P.127
Chapter 10	Soul Winning	P.136
Conclusion		P.151

DEDICATION

———⋈———

To give praise, honour,
glory to the Almighty God.
This book is dedicated to
God the Father,
God the Son,
and
God the Holy Spirit.
Without Him, this work would not
have been possible.
Thank you Lord!

ACKNOWLEDGEMENTS

This book would not have been completed without valuable input from a few special people whom God brought into my life, most especially my family, you are truly a blessing from God.

I would like to acknowledge the many authors whose books have over the years been invaluable sources of knowledge and inspiration to me.

My gratitude to everyone who will be affected by this book. May God bless you all In the Wonderful Name of Jesus Christ of Nazareth Amen.

ABOUT THE AUTHOR

―――⋈―――

Elizabeth L. Audu was born in Lagos, Nigeria, originated from Edo State (Ishan) Irua/Uromi, and is a former staff member of the Nigerian Television Authority (NTA), Victoria Island, Lagos. She has since lived in the United Kingdom for many years, as a Registered Nurse and Community Practitioner. Elizabeth holds a Diploma of Higher Education in Adult Nursing and degree in Bachelor of Science (Hons) in Health Promotion and Public Health. She is able to impact the community in promoting health and well-being of the family. She attained a Diploma in Christian Ministries at the National Open College Network and a degree in Bachelor of Arts in Pastoral Theology from Trinity College, at Newburgh in the State of Indiana, U.S.A. She is a Pastor, a motivational speaker, and a counsellor in the areas of prayers.

To purchase this book
Please contact:
07525852175
07534794826
07417577864
Email: Pstmrselizabethaudu@mail.com

INTRODUCTION

The title of this book, as indicated, was spoken during Jesus Christ's ministration on the Mount, and towards the end, while addressing His disciples, He focused precisely on two choices - the broad and the narrow gate. Although what is expected from the individual is to come through the narrow path that leads to eternal life (Matthew 7:13, 14):

13 Enter ye in at the strait gate: for wide is the gate, and broad is the way, that leadeth to destruction, and many there be which go in thereat:

14 Because strait is the gate, and narrow is the way, which leadeth unto life, and few there be that find it.

The ultimate mandate is when you do what God has demanded from you in obedience. This is not about research findings, but the gospel truth, because there is no other way to eternal life, for broad is that way that leads to destruction.

There are many people treading the broad way, thus deviating from Kingdom principles. Hence, the way that leads to God's Kingdom is so narrow that few individuals find it. May we discover and obtain the right of entry as we obey His commandment in Jesus' name.

Also, another version according to (Luke 13:24):

Strive to enter in at the strait gate: for many, I say unto you, will seek to enter in, and shall not be able.

"Strait" means "narrow". Jesus declared that it is only through this one way we may be saved. which is solely passing through Christ, and no other deity. He is the journey planner of our life, and all we need to do is to follow His instruction by doing His will as commanded; that will give you and me access to the Kingdom of Heaven, because Jesus is the only leading way (John 14:6):

Jesus saith unto him, I am the way, the truth, and the life: no man cometh unto the Father, but by me.

Jesus emphasised that He is the architect of mankind. Thus, He is the only way humanity can approach the Heavenly Father, through whom individuals can have intimacy with their Creator. Making it to Heaven is a choice, as you work out your salvation. There might be some hurdles along the way like distraction, fear, doubt, discouragement, temptation etc, which could be from families, friends or colleagues, because Kingdom values entail discipline and accountability. As you walk down this path you and I need routine self-examination, whereby you are determined to take precautions for yourself and be mindful if you have wronged or sinned against God or humankind (Romans 3: 23):

For all have sinned, and come short of the glory of God.

This implies commission or omission, thus doing things that you are not supposed to do as a believer and falling beyond the expected standard.

The event that took place in the Garden of Eden led to the fall of man due to disobedience (Genesis 3:1-13):

Now the serpent was more subtile than any beast of the field which the LORD God had made. And he said unto the woman, Yea, hath God said, Ye shall not eat of every tree of the garden?

2 *And the woman said unto the serpent, We may eat of the fruit of the trees of the garden:*

3 *But of the fruit of the tree which is in the midst of the garden, God hath said, Ye shall not eat of it, neither shall ye touch it, lest ye die.*

4 *And the serpent said unto the woman, Ye shall not surely die:*

5 *For God doth know that in the day ye eat thereof, then your eyes shall be opened, and ye shall be as gods, knowing good and evil.*

6 And when the woman saw that the tree was good for food, and that it was pleasant to the eyes, and a tree to be desired to make one wise, she took of the fruit thereof, and did eat, and gave also unto her husband with her; and he did eat.

7 And the eyes of them both were opened, and they knew that they were naked; and they sewed fig leaves together, and make themselves aprons,

8 And they heard the voice of the LORD God walking in the garden in the cool of the day: and Adam and his wife hid themselves from the presence of the LORD God amongst the trees of the garden.

9 And the LORD God called unto Adam, and said unto him, Where art thou?

10 And he said, I heard thy voice in the garden, and I was afraid, because I was naked; and I hid myself.

11 And he said, Who told thee that thou wast naked? Hast thou eaten of the tree, whereof I commanded thee that thou shouldest not eat?

12 And the man said, The woman whom thou gavest to be with me, she gave me of the tree, and I did eat.

13 And the LORD God said unto the woman, What is this that thou hast done? And the woman said, The serpent beguiled me, and I did eat.

Satan has planted a seed of doubt in the heart of man. Doubt is the absence of faith in the spiritual perspective. As he crept in, via craftiness, and deceived Eve, while she lured Adam to eat the forbidden fruit, this deflected man from the pre-planned agenda of God for mankind. Disobedience against God's commandment resulted in an unpleasant life that brought forth hard labour, pain, and death. This incident is telling the children of God not to deviate from the laid-down principles of God, because the end result is adversity. Adam and Eve were deprived of intimacy, thus losing a personal relationship with their God. The ultimate goal was destabilised, but they were driven out of the Garden by being displaced. Hence, that is how God rejects people who disobey His commandment and do not walk in the precept of God.

There are negative personalities embedded in Satan seeking whom he may devour. The spirit of Pride is of the devil, not from God. From the spiritual viewpoint, being proud is when someone possesses a disobedient personality negatively and does not comply with God's instruction, contrary to His commandment. Thus self-will is unacceptable for the Kingdom mandate. The above Scripture signifies that whenever God does anything, the devil always wanted to deploy an alternative strategy trying to regroup its cohort. Yet Satan is the originator of manipulation, pride, doubt, deceit, killing, betrayal, hypocrisy, idolatry, witchcraft, confusion, fear, etc.

Similarly, from the account of Prophet Isaiah in (Isaiah 14:12-23), verses 12-15:

12 *How art thou fallen from Heaven, O Lucifer, son of the morning how art thou cut down to the ground, which didst weaken the nations!*

13 For thou hast said in thine heart, I will ascend into Heaven, I will exalt my throne above the stars of God: I will sit also upon the mount of the congregation, in the sides of the north:

14 I will ascend above the heights of the clouds; I will be like the most High.

15 Yet thou shalt be brought down to hell, to the sides of the pit.

Lucifer, identified as Satan, created to be one of God's primary angels, was supposed to be an angel of light with many qualities, but disappointed his Creator; he was proud and arrogant as he wanted to lift himself above God. This issue was powerfully demonstrated and taught by Jesus Christ during His teaching amongst His ambitious disciples that true greatness is shown in humility. In Jesus' demonstration as a role model he worked on earth, in humility washed the feet of His disciples, welcomed little children, and willingly sacrificed His life to deliver man from the self-centred tyranny of sinful acts. Lucifer rebelled against God, and was ascribed by him as the initiator of sin, like a thief, deceiver, destroyer, murderer, etc.

However, his activities always oppose directives from God, falsifying agendas, even eradicating all the good work of God. Therefore, egotism that elevates itself against God, in anyone with a selfish lifestyle, will be unable to access the narrow path. His subtle nature with negative characteristics and its betrayal caused humanity to fall. As a result, for a believer not to dwell in sinful attributes that Satan had initiated, God vividly stated what He hates as the significant deadly types of sin in Proverbs 6: 16-19:

16 These six things doth the LORD hate; yea seven are an abomination unto him:

17 A proud look, a lying tongue, and hands that shed innocent blood.

18 A heart that deviseth wicked imaginations, feet that be swift in running to mischief,

19 A false witness that speaketh lies, and he that soweth discord among brethren.

God signifies the people He hates for their evil practices, as declared in verse 17. Lucifer was cast out, known as Satan due to his arrogance, with lying tongue, full of dubious devices acting wickedly, thereby shedding innocent blood. For example, King Herod executed an evil plan when Jesus was born, leading to the slaughter of all children under the age of two (Matthew 2:7-18). God is emphasising what an abomination this is to His doctrines. So, for anyone out there utilizing his/her position to terrorise people under their leadership, God is telling you that He dislikes it, so make the decision to change to moral practices because the Kingdom of Heaven is at hand.

Proverbs 6 Verse 18 quantified how a heart that devises wicked imagination has feet that are swift in running mischief. An example was a man in the name of King Saul (1st Samuel Chapters 19-23), who pursued King David with the intention to slay him but could not. This king tried several times to kill David, but because the hand of the Lord was with him, Saul could not prevail. The Lord hates these wicked acts, imploring anyone living against the mandate of God to turn from evil ways.

Proverbs 6 Verse 19 specified as false witness any person lying against his fellow brethren; he that soweth discord among members in Mark 14:56-57:

56 For many bare false witness against him, but their witness agreed not together.

57 And there arose certain, and bare false witness against him saying,

This incident took place when Jesus was brought before the high priest, without any fault but falsified allegations against the Lord. This type of scenario has led many people into imprisonment or captivity due to false witness, accusation and injustice. Brethren, God is raising an alert that none of those characteristics from the above account will inherit internal life, still less obtain access through the strait gate. Now it is time to embrace a change to godly living towards eternal life. Today is the day of salvation, while tomorrow might be too late. The thief was saved at the last minute on the cross. If Jesus could intercede for him, He can do likewise for you and me (Luke 23: 39-43). Did you realise that you cannot get anything from whomsoever you have dishonoured? Adam and Eve were originally created to worship God and honour Him, but that zeal was destroyed by Satan. The thief that had no hope with the intention of ending up in hell was narrowly saved at the last minute. God is merciful and compassionate.

However, there are occasions when the narrow-minded man knew how to do good but failed to do so due to his sinful nature, and was unable to live up to the required standard as demanded from God. Jesus is the true light of the world. He came to redeem humanity from all sinful deeds. No wonder Apostle Paul established in Romans 7:14-20 New International version:

14 We know that the law is spiritual; but I am unspiritual, sold as a slave to sin.

15 I do not understand what I do. For what I want to do I do not do, but what I hate I do. 16 And If I do what I do not want to do, I agree that the law is good.

17 As it is, it is no longer I myself who do it, but it is sin living in me.

18 I know that nothing good lives in me, that is, in my sinful nature. For I have the desire to do what is good, but I cannot carry it out.

19 For what I do is not the good I want to do; no, the evil I do not want to do – this I keep on doing.

20 Now if I do what I do not want to do, it is no longer I who do it, but it is sin living in me that does it.

From the New Testament perspectives, Apostle Paul demonstrated how sin has perverted him when he desired to do good as God has commanded, but somehow along the line he could not do it. Whenever he intended to do right, nature opposed it. Thus he struggled as a believer to keep the law. This is applicable to all believers, because there are various occasions when we experience the kind of struggle Apostle Paul was trying to explain. By the Spirit of the Living God we are beyond condemnation, because Christ died and is risen for our salvation and nothing will be able to separate us from the love of God in Christ Jesus.

This tells anyone who acknowledges sin to confess it to God, and to ensure that same sin is not repeated. He is a just and merciful God. It was when the prodigal Son did come to himself, in awareness of his sin, against God and his father with inner conviction that he had a turnaround (Luke 15:11-24). Therefore, God is looking for someone like Job, Joseph, Abraham etc, righteous men and women who did not allow the flesh to overrule their lives. The Lord is beckoning for repentance, so hating sin is enough to turn from ill habits.

As many as I love, I rebuke and chasten: be zealous therefore, and repent. God only chastises those whom He loves. Jesus Christ has given us the Holy Ghost's power to help us during our time of trouble, depending on the power that rules you within. We are created to worship our Creator, and those that worship Him do it in truth and in spirit. As you work in God there is no law nor condemnation that can control your life; it is only for you and me to treat others as you intended to be treated. When you do His will, no evil shall befall you, and if any does, He will fight your battle. He is an impartial God.

Consequently, to assess this narrow gate there are standardized paths that need to be adhered to. This book came into being in an act of obedience and strictly by the word of knowledge. As we strive to do His will, may we reign with our

Heavenly Father at the end of this race, Amen. Be inspired as you read.

What are the criteria for entry to the narrow gate?

Some of the required standards of living in harmony to the Heavenly mandate are as follows: to be obedient to God's commandment, to live in a holy and righteous manner, not to be hypocritical. To be able to crucify the flesh, not to be proud, to be born again, having the heart of forgiveness, filled with the Holy Spirit, fear of the Lord. Also to observe fasting and prayer, as this is the key to resolve issues of life, to have faith and believe in God via His Words, which is the opposite of doubt. Also to show kindness with the love of Christ to be charitable, and soul-winning (evangelism).

There is no proud individual with a negative personality who finds abode in the Kingdom of Heaven. Hence, it is better to take precautions in whatever you do, and to regularly make an effort to undergo self-assessment if you are living according to God's standards. It is not enough to be a leader in any organisation nor within the house of God but relatively, to be a good role model to your generation, either within the secular or the spiritual world. God is the regulator of the whole earth. The disciples of Christ emulated Him as they went about making disciples and ministering with signs and wonders, and many souls were added to the congregation. Their way of life portrayed Christ, hence they were recognised as followers of Jesus and were referred to "Christians". Antioch was the first place the disciples were recognised as followers of Christ (Act 11:26):

And when he had found him, he brought him unto Antioch. And it came to pass, that a whole year they assembled themselves with the church, and taught much people. And the disciples were called Christians first in Antioch.

The lifestyles of Christ's Disciples portrayed whom they proclaimed. The name 'Christian' was initially an offensive word within their community when referring to the followers of Jesus Christ. For that reason, it is applicable at this contemporary era, which is still an ongoing issue due to rigour, or political correctness. It is a little daunting when sharing or making an effort to introduce Christ to your colleagues, friends or members of your extended families, but in most instances one is being restrained. Nonetheless, as a result of regulations and constraints, there are some behaviours that were tied up in something similar to self-righteousness, slothfulness or living a double standard way of life that is contrary to divinity, while the path towards the narrow gate could only be achieved in total submission to His mandates.

Chapter One

GOD'S COMMANDMENT

Therefore, we should strive to love one another, even the unlovable. As a believer, it is mandatory to make every effort to do greater things for the Lord, if it entails going the extra mile for others. We emulate Christ by going all the way preaching the Word of God, and do His will as instructed according to His decree. There is huge expectation from everyone who will make it to eternal life via the narrow gate which is a required standard. For that reason, children of God, we seek for his divine will that will enhance our journey to the Heavenly Kingdom.

There are laid-down guidelines within the Ten Commandment context as stated in Exodus 20: 1-17:

1   And God spake all these words, saying,

2   I am the LORD thy God, which have brought thee out of the land of Egypt, out of the house of bondage.

3   Thou shalt have no other gods before me.

4   Thou shalt not make unto thee any graven image, or any likeness of any thing that is in Heaven above, or that is in the earth beneath, or that is in the water under the earth:

5   Thou shalt not bow down thyself to them, nor serve them: for I the LORD thy God am a jealous God, visiting the iniquity of the fathers upon the children unto the third and fourth generation of them that hate me;

6 *And showing mercy unto thousands of them that love me, and keep my commandments.*

7 *Thou shalt not take the name of the LORD thy God in vain: for the LORD will not hold him guiltless that taketh his name in vain.*

8 *Remember the Sabbath day, to keep it holy.*

9 *Six days shalt thou labor, and do all thy work:*

10 *But the seventh day is the Sabbath of the LORD thy God: in it thou shalt not do any work, thou, nor thy son, nor thy daughter, thy manservant, nor thy maidservant, nor thy cattle, nor thy stranger that is within thy gates.*

11 *For in six days the LORD made Heaven and earth, the sea, and all that in them is, and rested the seventh day: wherefore the LORD blessed the Sabbath day, and hallowed it.*

12 Honour thy father and thy mother: that thy days may be long upon the land which the LORD thy God giveth thee.

13 Thou shalt not kill.

14 Thou shalt not commit adultery

15 Thou shalt not steal.

16 Thou shalt not bear false witness against thy neighbour:

17 Thou shalt not covet thy neighbour's house, thou shalt not covet thy neighbour's wife, nor his manservants, nor his maidservant, nor his ox, nor his ass, nor any thing that is thy neighbour's.

The above designated rules ordered by God are self-explanatory for humanity to follow. The Creator of Heaven and earth expects gratification from mankind. He was reminding His people how He brought them out of Egyptian bondage. Hence we all are His handiwork, with no obligation other than to serve and worship Him only, because there is no God like Him. He also emphasised that He is jealous. We must have no deity, no idol except to revere the only true God. We should love one another, even all their assets. Someone with a loving personality cannot plot evil against their fellow human being. That is the full gospel of Jesus as declared by God John 3:16:

For God so loved the world, that he gave his only begotten Son, that whosoever believeth in him should not perish, but have everlasting life.

Love is an attribute of God that portrayed His Sovereignty power. It is unconditional and reliable. The sinless Christ redeemed the souls of humanity by a sacrificial offering on the Cross of Calvary. What a Mighty God who cares for His creatures.

Furthermore, Psalms 81:9-10 demonstrates the word of God that:

*9 **There shall no strange god be in thee; neither shalt thou worship any strange god.***

*10 **I am the LORD thy God, which brought thee out of the land of Egypt: open thy mouth wide, and I will fill it.***

The instruction is a rule that governed mankind, that no deity, either genuine or fabricated, can have any contention with the true God. He demands a personal relationship with Him which is an important tool to service. We are created to worship, honour and adore Him likewise (Psalms 63:1-7), emphasised in the following verses:

1. *O God, thou art my God; early will I seek thee: my soul thirsteth for thee, my flesh longeth for thee in a dry and thirsty land, where no water is;*

2. *To see thy power and thy glory, so as I have seen thee in the sanctuary.*

3. *Because thy loving-kindness is better than life, my lips shall praise thee.*

4. *Thus will I bless thee while I live: I will lift up my hands in thy name.*

5. *My soul shall be satisfied as with marrow and fatness; and my mouth shall praise thee with joyful lips;*

6. *When I remember thee upon my bed, and meditate on thee in the night watches.*

7 *Because thou hast been my help, therefore in the shadow of thy wings will I rejoice.*

This is a thanksgiving and appreciating psalm when King David was going through the challenges of life. Whatever circumstances you and I might be passing through, the Lord is making a demand that we should engage in a thankful attitude, though it is not so easy. That is what the Lord requested from you as a believer. Thereby, your intention, your love for God, will be X-rayed and your faith in God affirmed.

The question is, if you are confronted by any issue of life, He is in charge. He provides a way of escape, as we have faith and belief. Our body is the temple of God, and is not meant to be polluted by any illicit drugs, with notions of alternative solutions to problems. Do not
live an unrighteous lifestyle, or lose hope. God tests our faith so that we may trust His faithfulness. You were created in His own image, in His likeness, to worship, to appreciate Him. Thus your expression of gratitude for what He has done, is doing and is about to do in your life.

Despite all odds, you and I need to trust in God as you boldly confess your sins and honour Him by your worshipping, for that is the ultimate goal. He lives in you always and never forsakes you, because your body is His dwelling place (Matthew 21: 12-17):

And Jesus went into the temple of God, and cast out all them that sold and bought in the temple, and overthrew the tables of the money changers, and the seats of them that sold doves,

13 And said unto them, It is written, MY HOUSE SHALL BE CALLED THE HOUSE OF PRAYER; but ye have made it a DEN OF THIEVES.

14 And the blind and the lame came to him in the temple; and be healed them.

15 And when the chief priests and scribes saw the wonderful things that he did, and the children crying in the temple, and saying, Hosanna to the son of David; they were sore displeased.

16 And said unto him, Hearest thou what these say? And Jesus saith unto them, Yea; have ye never read, OUT OF THE MOUTHS OF BABES AND SUCKLINGS THOU HAST PERFECTED PRAISE?

17 And he left them, and went out of the city into Bethany; and he lodged there.

Our body is the temple of the Most High God, created to worship and to serve Him. Although a sinful nature is to some extent responsible for blindfolding people's feelings and thoughts, depriving them of beholding spiritual things and unrighteousness could have no place. No wonder! It was demonstrated from the account of King David in 2nd Samuel 11:3, 4:

3 And David sent and inquired after the woman. And one said, Is not this Bathsheba, the daughter of Eliam, the wife of Uriah the Hittite?

4 And David sent messengers, and took her, and she came in unto him, and he lay with her; for she was purified from her uncleanness: and she returned unto her house.

This scenario was after David ordered Uriah to the front line, where he was killed, and he married Bathsheba. The child conceived in adultery died, but was rebuked by the Prophet of God. God blessed them with other children, and Solomon was amongst the four. This sinful act led David into fasting and praying for days, pleading for forgiveness in sincerity from his heart. He was rebuked by God through His Prophet. It was then Psalm 51 came into being, giving expression to why he was attributed to David as a man after God's own heart.

1 Have mercy upon me, O God, according to thy loving kindness: according unto the multitude of thy tender mercies blot out my transgressions.

2 Wash me thoroughly from mine iniquity, and cleanse me from my sin.

3 For I acknowledge my transgressions: and my sin is ever before me.

4 Against thee, thee only, have I sinned, and done this evil in thy sight: that thou mightiest be justified when thou speakest, and be clear when thou judgest.

5 Behold, I was shapen in iniquity, and in sin did my mother conceive me.

6 Behold, thou desirest truth in the inward parts: and in the hidden part thou shalt make me to know wisdom.

7 Purge me with hyssop, and I shall be clean: wash me, and I shall be whiter than snow.

8 Make me to hear joy and gladness; that the bones which thou hast broken may rejoice.

9 Hide thy face from my sins, and blot out all mine iniquities.

10 Create in me a clean heart, O God; and renew a right spirit within me.

11 Cast me not away from thy presence; and take not thy Holy Spirit from me.

12 Restore unto me the joy of thy salvation; and uphold me with thy free spirit.

13 Then will I teach transgressors thy ways; and sinners shall be converted unto thee.

14 Deliver me from bloodguiltiness, O God, thou God of my salvation: and my tongue shall sing aloud of thy righteousness.

15 O Lord, open thou my lips; and my mouth shall show forth thy praise.

16 For thou desirest not sacrifice; else would I give it: thou delightest not in burnt offering.

17 The sacrifices of God are a broken spirit: a broken and a contrite heart, O God, thou wilt not despise.

18 Do good in thy good pleasure unto Zion: build thou the walls of Jerusalem.

19 Then shalt thou be pleased with the sacrifices of righteousness, with burnt offering and whole burnt offering: then shall they offer bullocks upon thine altar.

King David was a man of flesh and blood like you and me, but he was sensitive towards sin, which few people take into consideration. Whenever he wronged God, he quickly acknowledged his weakness and sought forgiveness. He knew how to appease God. The above psalm was established, teaching and addressing the issues in regard to when David failed and messed up with another man's wife (Uriah). To this extent he shed innocent blood. He had already breached the commandment of God. So God is advocating that everyone who has sinned against God and humanity in one capacity or the other should confess their sins, because He is full of compassion. In His Sovereignty and mercy all you have to do is let it come from within to confess your sin: inner conviction.

Let's ponder on the first two verses, that was when he forwarded his supplication seeking for forgiveness from God. While in verse 3 he was confessing his guilt, he obtained spiritual cleansing for total restoration, which is applicable to everyone who has sinned against God but needs to come in humility for repentance so that you can be useful towards the service of God. For you to be restored by acknowledging your sin and seeking for pardon as God did for David He will do it for you. A significant example was about the lost son (Luke 15: 11-24):

11 And he said, A certain man had two sons:

12 And the younger of them said to his father, Father, give me the portion of goods that falleth to me. And he divided unto them his living.

13 And not many days after the younger son gathered all together, and took his journey into a far country, and there wasted his substance with riotous living.

14 And when he had spent all, there arose a mighty famine in that land; and he began to be in want.

15 And he went and joined himself to a citizen of that country; and he sent him into his fields to feed swine.

16 And he would fain have filled his belly with the husks that the swine did eat: and no man gave unto him.

17 And when he came to himself, he said, How many hired servants of my father's have bread enough and to spare, and I perish with hunger!

18 I will arise and go to my father, and will say unto him, Father, I have sinned against Heaven, and before thee.

19 And am no more worthy to be called thy son: make me as one of thy hired servants.

20 And he arose, and came to his father. But when he was yet a great way off, his father saw him, and had compassion, and ran, and fell on his neck, and kissed him.

21 And the son said unto him, Father, I have sinned against Heaven, and in thy sight, and am no more worthy to be called thy son.

22 But the father said to his servants, Bring forth the best robe, and put it on him; and put a ring on his hand, and shoes on his feet:

23 And bring hither the fatted calf, and kill it; and let us eat and be merry:

24 For this my son was dead, and is alive again; he was lost, and is found. And they began to be merry.

In verse 17, after squandering all the resources, the young man lost his integrity and came to his senses. Thus he remembered his birth-right. It was better for him to go back to his father than to die in a foreign land where he could not be located.

As he said, "How many hired servants of my father have bread enough and to spare, and I perish with hunger". He returned home with genuine repentance, but his father in an act of love graciously accepted him. Instantaneously he was restored. God knows your intention; not what you intended to eat or drink but what comes out of your heart. Your life will never remain the same, but supernaturally be transformed by encountering the power of the Holy Spirit (illumination). It does not matter the nature of your sin; if you determine to confess and turn from it as the prodigal son did. Hence, God is calling on sinners to do away with sin, obey His commandment, do His will, and live a holy life that gives access to the narrow gate. Our Maker is merciful, ready to embrace you and replace you back in your original position. He is ready to welcome any of His children that were once lost but are now found back into His Kingdom.

Nonetheless, we have been given a gift of no condemnation as recorded when Jesus forgives an adulteress (John 8:3-11):

3 And the scribes and Pharisees brought unto him a woman taken in adultery; and when they had set her in the midst,

4 They say unto him, Master, this woman was taken in adultery, in the very act.

5 Now Moses in the law commanded us, that such should be stoned: but what sayest thou?

6 This they said, tempting him, that they might have to accuse him. But Jesus stooped down, and with his finger wrote on the ground, as though he heard them not.

7 So when they continued asking him, he lifted up himself, and said unto them, He that is without sin among you, let him first cast a stone at her.

8 And again he stooped down, and wrote on the ground.

9 And they which heart it, being convicted by their own conscience, went out one by one, beginning at the eldest, even unto the last: and Jesus was left alone, and the woman standing in the midst.

10 When Jesus had lifted up himself, and saw none but the woman, he said unto her, Woman where are those thine accusers? hath no man condemned thee?

11 She said, No man, Lord. And Jesus said unto her, Neither do I condemn thee: go, and sin no more.

The above verses, specifically verses 10-11, stated that the scribes and Pharisees were seeking to find fault in Jesus, to see whether He would advocate the law or support the sinner. To their surprise, when Jesus lifted himself up from the writing on the floor, He inquired from the woman where her fault-finders were. If anyone among them had never sinned they should be the first to cast a stone. Surprisingly, the complainers dropped their stones and turned their backs. Jesus was the only one who could have condemned this woman, but instead he instructed her to sin no more. He is addressing believers also, that whatever gravity of sin you must have engulfed yourself, your sole duty is to confess and never to be repeated anymore. The Lord is the supernatural one and only who can forgive sins. It does not matter what type of negative lifestyle you have entangled yourself in, but it is a new dawn in Christ Jesus as stated by Apostle Paul, who was once an accuser of the brethren, and boldly declared in the following verses (2nd Corinthians 7:1-2):

Having therefore these promises, dearly beloved, let us cleanse ourselves from all filthiness of the flesh and spirit, perfecting holiness in the fear of God.

2 Receive us; we have wronged no man, we have corrupted no man, we have defrauded no man.

Apostle Paul was reassuring and demonstrating during his ministry, declaring boldly according to the above verses that the Corinthians should refuse to be linked with evil practices but solely be committed to Christ as He demands from them: the purification from every sinful lifestyle that can contaminates their lives. Rather, better living righteously in Godly fear. Although, Paul's relationship with the Corinthians has conveyed both discomfort and sorrowfulness during his motivational exaltation but was beneficial with positive outcome, while they changed from their old pathways. The same is applicable to believers at this period *because* you cannot judge anyone by their past, but to be encouraged towards having a personal relationship with God.

Furthermore, you do not attempt to judge, for God is the only judge. Apostle Paul himself was a former persecutor, and now his life has been transformed by the Power of the Holy Ghost, because old things have passed away, as illustrated in 2nd Corinthians 5: 17:

Therefore if any man be in Christ, he is a new creature: old things are passed away; behold, all things are become new.

The only way forward is just for a sinner to make up their mind, by declaration of guilt of sin while God in His mercy is ready to welcome back His truant son/daughter. As Apostle Paul recognises that his assignment is of reconciliation, therefore from that perspective, to bring back the life of his followers, for those that have gone astray to the perfect will of God with the inner conviction of Jesus dwelling in their heart. Hence, yours is to minister to someone, it is God who deals with the mind for conviction towards salvation.

No wonder! God declared that David was a man after His own heart. God is dealing with your inner mind, not your outward appearance. We should strive to walk according to His precepts to access the eternal Kingdom via the narrow path.

Although the stated commandment cannot be achieved without the love of God, which is self-explanatory and is embedded in the New Testament context according to (John 3:16):

For God so loved the world, that he gave his only begotten Son, that whosoever believeth in him should not perish, but have everlasting life.

Chapter Two

LOVE

When you show love, being good to one another, the negative aspects of the ten commandments can never happen. Love is the pathway towards the Straitened Entry, beginning from Exodus 20: 1-17, as stated in this book according to the Scripture. When you care, showing kindness, love your neighbour as yourself as Jesus established (John 15:12):

This is my commandment, That ye love one another, as I have loved you.

The Word of the Lord declared that as Christians we are called to show others love.

Jesus expressed to His disciples, to dwell in agreement, in one accord, cooperatively to operate as instructed from the apostolic doctrine that produces good results. According to the book of Luke 6:20-38, Jesus pointed towards the beatitudes from the verses below emphasised solely on compassion, but His mode of teaching is always in parables.

20 And he lifted up his eyes on his disciples, and said, Blessed be ye poor: for yours is the Kingdom of God.

21 Blessed are ye that hunger now: for ye shall be filled. Blessed are ye that weep now: for ye shall laugh.

22 Blessed are ye, when men shall hate you, and when they shall separate you from their company, and shall reproach you, and cast out your name as evil, for the Son of man's sake.

23 Rejoice ye in that day, and leap for joy: for, behold, your reward is great in Heaven: for in the like manner did their fathers unto the prophets.

24 But woe unto you that are rich! For ye have received your consolation.

25 Woe unto you that are full for ye shall hunger. Woe unto you that laugh now! For ye shall mourn and weep

26 Woe unto you, when all men shall speak well of you! For so did their fathers to the false prophets.

This was encouraging and reassuring to anyone who has decided to follow Jesus as commanded, despite past experience such as poverty, or undergoing hunger or persecution, either being falsely accused because of the faithfulness of sharing the Good News of Christ. Yet you are advised to be kind, have compassion and be loving to one another because a reward awaits you. Nevertheless, you and I do have a reason for rejoicing, for whatever you do for the sake of the Kingdom will never be in vain. The internal Kingdom could only be accessed via the straitened entry and is strictly in total conformity to the will of God.

27 But I say unto you which hear, Love your enemies, do good to them which hate you,

28 Bless them that curse you, and pray for them which despitefully use you.

29 And unto him that smiteth thee on the one cheek offer also the other; and him that taketh away thy cloak forbid not to take thy coat also.

31 Give to every man that asketh of thee; and of him that taketh away thy goods ask them not again.

32 And as ye would that men should do to you, do ye also to them likewise.

33 For if ye love them which love you, what thank have ye? For sinners also love those that love them.

34 And if ye do good to them which do good to you, what thank have ye? For sinners also do even the same.

35 And if ye lend to them of whom ye hope to receive, what thank have ye? for sinners also lend to sinners, to receive as much again.

36 But love ye your enemies, and do good, and lend, hoping for nothing again; and your reward shall be great, and ye shall

be the children of the Highest: for he is kind unto the unthankful and to the evil.

36 Be ye therefore merciful, as your Father also is merciful.

The above verses demonstrate the teaching of Jesus. You and I are to do likewise, to be good ambassadors to emulate Christ, portrayed in doing good as servants of God. Still He continues in His teaching that we should show love to our enemies, which is a sign of spiritual achievement, because Jesus placed a great priority on mankind, as we are in the likeness of God. He emphasised that believers should make every effort to do good to those who hate you. Jesus says we are to model our relationships on God, who is merciful and kind to the ungrateful and the wicked. There are some people who are difficult to deal with, yet Jesus demonstrated the 'agape' love and encouraged us to love the unlovable. Furthermore, He required us to show kindness to the underprivileged, not only to those that can pay us back. As you and I extend the hand of charity, God who perceived behind the scenes will in return grant you an eternal reward. Additionally, on these other two verses that:

37 Judge not, and ye shall not be judged: condemn not, and ye shall not be condemned: forgive, and ye shall be forgiven:

38 Give, and it shall be given unto you; good measure, pressed down, and shaken together, and running over, shall men give into your bosom. For with the same measure that ye mete withal it shall be measured to you again.

Warning against the dominant condemnation of others is the duty of God alone; only He can execute any judgment. However, to forgive one another is mandatory. Therefore, relationships with others are to be free of judging thus (non-judgemental), and filled with forgiveness (Romans 14: 1-13).

Also we endeavour to give love in action, as God did first. Hence, the unbelievers can become Christian through your lifestyle by sharing the love of Christ. So you and I have no choice other than to assist and support in diverse ways, for example, to give your talent, like singing, dancing, cooking or playing music, which is therapeutic, or you can spare some time for home visiting, giving resources or making a short phone call, not for gossiping, but rather to give words of encouragement, just to make an impact on someone's life. Your testimony can encourage and transform someone's life by sharing a message of hope with the hopeless. We all need to pray for divine direction to acknowledge where help is needed within the gathering of brethren. There are instances when you might perceive that all you have is a little trash in your hand, like that widow with the little jar of oil, who became the solver of her problems when she shared her burden with Prophet Elisha (2nd Kings 4:1-7). Moreover, to emulate and abide to His Laws stated in John 13:35:

By this shall all men know that ye are my disciples, if ye have love one to another.

Many perceived love as a feeling, but this is not so, because the book of John (1st John 4:8) says: ***He that loveth not knoweth not God; for God is love.***

The true love of God signifies action. Whatever you do is done unto God who is a rewarder, because you might be thinking that a token gift is just too little, but it could be a luxury to another person that needs support. We need to pray for God to open our eyes, giving supernatural illumination and to be sensitive to things of the spirit for you to acknowledge who needs assistance within the household of faith, even within your environment.

There is behaviour that is unacceptable in the forum of God, like gossiping, backbiting, lies, hypocrisy etc. This behaviour has led many believers to avoid discussing or relating to anyone within the body of Christ, or talk about personal issues. Therefore, from various perspectives a lot of people are suffering depression, because love is wanting. Our love for Jesus needs to be reflected in our way of life towards one another even those who may be unlovable because it is obligatory by God. When you love, there would not be evil plan neither negative plot, nor hatred, even betrayal of trust as Judas Iscariot betrayed Jesus (Matthew 26:14-16):

14 Then one of the twelve, called Judas Iscariot, went unto the chief priests,

15 And said unto them, What will ye give me, and I will deliver him unto you? And they covenanted with him for thirty pieces of silver.

16 And from that time he sought opportunity to betray him.

What happened to Jesus has happened to many believers, either within the gathering of brethren, the family, the workplace, even within the secular world. Many outrages that are against the will of God are out there. Jesus Christ was betrayed by one of His disciples. What was his achievement? In the end, he lost his soul for nothing because of envy and being a men pleaser. Therefore, it is better for you not to perish because of vain things and materialism. It is advisable to try and change from evil malpractice before it is too late. Broad is that way that led to destruction, you should build towards the strait access to internal life, where there will be no sorrow, and no problems. Remembering that the wages of sin is death, then what would be the gain in inheriting the whole world and losing your precious soul. God forbid!

On the contrary, if there is any indication of deceit, it would not yield a pleasant outcome; that was what happened at the events demonstrated by the move of the Holy Spirit in Acts 5:1-11:

1 But a certain man named Ananias, with Sapphira his wife, sold a possession,

2 And kept back part of the price, his wife also being privy to it, and brought a certain part, and laid it at the apostle's feet.

3 But Peter said, Ananias, why hath Satan filled thine heart to lie to the Holy Ghost, and to keep back part of the price of the land?

4 While it remained, was it not thine own? And after it was sold, was it not in thine own power? Why hast thou conceived this thing in thine heart? thou hast not lied unto men, but unto God.

5 And Ananias hearing these words fell down, and gave up the ghost: and great fear came on all them that heard these things.

6 And the young men arose, wound him up, and carried him out, and buried him.

7 And it was about the space of three hours after, when his wife, not knowing what was done, came in.

8 And Peter answered unto her, Tell me whether ye sold the land for so much? And she said, Yea, for so much.

9 Then Peter said unto her, How is it that ye have agreed together to tempt the Spirit of the Lord? behold, the feet of them which have buried thy husband are at the door, and shall carry thee out.

10 Then fell she down straightway at his feet, and yielded up the ghost: and the young men came in, and found her dead, and, carrying her forth, buried her by her husband.

11 And great fear came upon all the church, and upon as many as heard these things.

Ananias and Sapphira were husband and wife, but the mysticism of the Holy Spirit was evidently proven. Ananias lied to the Spirit of God, and was ignorant that they were not dealing with a carnal being but Divinity. Any faithful man or woman of God officiating in the realm of the power of the Holy Ghost as assigned accordingly, is representing God, not acting of their own accord. From the above episode, it was a voluntary pledge that was not compulsory for communal sharing which was the usual practice in order to support the needy within their midst. Ananias' sin was not because of keeping back some portion of what he had sold, but because of his insincerity. God does not judge every believer's sin with death, although in some circumstances He does. Ananias deceitfully agreed with his wife, Sapphira, and the same power of the Holy Spirit struck the wife dead. Both of them have no passion nor love their fellowmen but rather left a bad and negative legacy for their family, the body of Christ and their community, but this is for our warning and to learn from mistakes that God still reigns in the affairs of men; He owns the universe. What shall it profit a man to gain the whole world but lose his/her soul? As believers it is better to choose the right path and to be totally disciplined towards God's commandment, showing love towards others that leads to life everlasting.

On the other hand, it is important for us to be in unity, oneness, in togetherness to effectively fulfil the Law of God because iron sharpens iron; we need one another for effective productivity. However, negative attributes such as envy, jealousy and hypocrisy lured Judas to betray his Master. There are many people that have betrayed their loved ones, a husband betraying his wife or vice versa, managers betraying their staff and vice versa, etc. It happens within the spiritual and secular worlds, even globally. We need to turn back to God and seek forgiveness; our God is sovereign and merciful. If you love what your neighbour is doing, it would be advisable to draw closer to him/her by making friends and having a good relationship that will give the opportunity to ask questions about the way forward, how help could be rendered. Also, when you take a bold step you make a demand from God's direction. God sees your heart's desire, and when you make a request, He will answer. He is a prayer-answering God.

Furthermore, if you need to enhance yourself in terms of education, why not take the step? Do it – there is no age limit/barrier – or get someone to put you through rather than putting yourself down with low self-esteem, or tearing other people down. All these little foxes could have a negative impact towards making Heaven, and they are disastrous. Please, before you overreact to any circumstances, just realise that you brought nothing and go with nothing, it is all down to vanity. The Kingdom of Heaven is the ultimate goal, Let's strive hard to get there.

Hebrew 13:8 Jesus Christ the same yesterday, and today, and forever.

Still, the way forward to eternal life: is all about total dedication in doing the perfect will of God (Romans 12:1-21):

1. *I beseech you therefore, brethren, by the mercies of God, that ye present your bodies a living sacrifice, holy, acceptable unto God, which is your reasonable service.*

2. *And be not conformed to this world: but be ye transformed by the renewing of your mind, that ye may prove what is that good, and acceptable, and perfect will of God.*

3 For I say, through the grace given unto me, to every man that is among you, not to think of himself more highly than he ought to think: but to think soberly, according as God hath dealt to every man the measure of faith.

4 For as we have many members in one body, and all members have not the same office:

5 So we, being many, are one body in Christ, and every one members one of another.

6 Having then gifts differing according to the grace that is given to us, whether prophecy, let us prophesy according to the proportion of faith;

7 Or ministry, let us wait on our ministering: or he that teacheth, on teaching:

8 Or he that exhorteth, on exhortation: he that giveth, let him do it with simplicity; he that ruleth, with diligence; he that showeth mercy, with cheerfulness.

9 Let love be without dissimulation. Abhor that which is evil; cleave to that which is good.

10 Be kindly affectioned one to another with brotherly love; in honour preferring one another;

11 Not slothful in business; fervent in spirit; serving the Lord;

12 Rejoicing in hope; patient in tribulation; continuing instant in prayer;

13 Distributing to the necessity of saints; given to hospitality.

14 Bless them which persecute you: bless, and curse not.

15 Rejoice with them that do rejoice, and weep with them that weep.

16 Be of the same mind one toward another. Mind not high things, but condescend to men of low estate. Be not wise in your own conceits.

17 Recompense to no man evil for evil. Provide things honest in the sight of all men.

18 If it be possible, as much as lieth in you, live peaceably with all men.

19 Dearly beloved, avenge not yourselves, but rather give place unto wrath: for it is written, VENGEANCE IS MINE: I WILL REPAY, saith the Lord.

20 THEREFORE IF THINE ENEMY HUNGER, FEED HIM; IF HE THIRST, GIVE HIM DRINK: FOR IN SO DOING THOU SHALT HEAP COALS OF FIRE ON HIS HEAD.

21 Be not overcome of evil, but overcome evil with good.

This was the demonstration for believers to live a righteous life, as Apostle Paul was stressing in this particular chapter that it is only God who has the right to avenge. As we work our way of salvation for the perfect will of God, never stop doing good. It is one thing to share the word of God, but be aware that there are some less privileged within your environment. Saints of God, let's ponder a little bit: within the Western world, especially Great Britain, they are able to practise and execute charity organisations, the social services etc, within the community to reach out to people who are unable, either due to lack of a job, or health-related concerns, even some asylum seekers depending on their statutes within the country. This is the Kingdom Agenda. It is one thing for us to pray and counsel people; it is another to practise what the Bible demands. As you give unto the poor you are lending unto the Lord. God is relational. Your neighbour is a family; it could be anyone within your reach. Therefore, brethren, let us endeavour to demonstrate love in action, for God is love. Hence, it was confirmed in Leviticus 19:18:

Thou shalt not avenge, nor bear any grudge against the children of thy people, but thou shalt love thy neighbour as thyself: I am the LORD.

Love in action is the most crucial guiding tenet in dealings with your neighbours, even their possessions, supporting the needy, showing kindness to others, and being honest in relationships with humanity at large. All these are embedded in the love of Christ. So also, God constructively made a demand from the account book of Isaiah 58:6-12:

6 *Is not this the fast that I have chosen? To loose the bands of wickedness, to undo the heavy burdens, and to let the oppressed go free, and that ye break every yoke?*

7 *Is it not to deal thy bread to the hungry, and that thou bring the poor that are cast out to thy house? when thou seest the naked, that thou cover him; and that thou hide not thyself from thine own flesh?*

8 *Then shall thy light break forth as the morning, and thine health shall spring forth speedily and thy righteousness shall go before thee; the glory of the LORD shall be thy rearward.*

9 *Then shalt thou call, and the LORD shall answer; thou shalt cry and he shall say, Here I am. If thou take away from the midst of thee the yoke, the putting forth of the finger, and speaking vanity;*

10 And if thou draw out thy soul to the hungry, and satisfy the afflicted soul: then shall thy light rise in obscurity, and thy darkness be as the noonday:

11 And the LORD shall guide thee continually, and satisfy thy soul in drought, and make fat thy bones; and thou shalt be like a watered garden, and like a spring of water, whose waters fail not.

12 And they that shall be of thee shall build the old waste places: thou shalt raise up the foundations of many generations; and thou shalt be called, The repairer of the breach, The restorer of paths to dwell in.

Fasting is a mode of discipline involving abstaining from food for scriptural exercises, in conjunction with prayers. But, this is not enough, as affirmed by God through His prophet Isaiah; Christianity can never be completed nor separated from compassion. Thus be loving, compassionate for the deprived, as instructed by God through the verses. So also, concerning societal fairness. Hereafter, Jesus is making a demand for believers to put into practice love in action, not only reading about it on paper but in doing it, for your fasting and prayer to be accepted. In the New Testament Jesus confirmed whatever you and I did to the least of our brothers and sisters that is solely what you did unto Him, when He was hungry, thirsty, naked. Whether homeless, in prison, with problems, you came to his rescue. Then when asked how and when, Jesus responded, in as much you can come to the aid of others, do the same unto Him.

Matthew 25:31-46:

31 When the Son of man shall come in his glory, and all the holy angels with him, then shall he sit upon the throne of his glory.

32 And before him shall be gathered all nations: and he shall separate them one from another, as a shepherd divideth his sheep from the goats'

33 And he shall set the sheep on his right hand, but the goats on the left.

34 Then shall the King say unto them on his right hand, Come, ye blessed of my Father, inherit the Kingdom prepared for you from the foundation of the world:

35 For I was hungered, and ye gave me meat: I was thirsty, and ye gave me drink: I was a stranger, and ye took me in:

36 Naked, and ye clothed me: I was sick, and ye visited me: I was in prison, and ye came unto me.

37 Then shall the righteous answer him, saying, Lord, when saw we thee an hungered, and fed thee? or thirsty, and gave thee drink?

38 When saw we thee a stranger, and took thee in? or naked, and clothed thee?

39 Or when saw we thee sick, or in prison, and came unto thee?

40 And the King shall answer and say unto them, Verily I say unto you, Inasmuch as ye have done it unto one of the least of these my brethren, ye have done it unto me.

41 Then shall he say also unto them on the left hand, Depart from me, ye cursed, into everlasting fire, prepared for the devil and his angels:

42 For I was an hungered, and ye gave me no meat: I was thirsty, and ye gave me no drink.

43 I was a stranger, and ye took me not in: naked, and ye clothed me not: sick, and in prison, and ye visited me not.

44 Then shall they also answer him, saying, Lord, when saw we thee an hungered, or athirst, or a stranger, or naked, or sick, or in prison, and did not minister unto thee?

45 Then shall he answer them, saying, Verily I say unto you, Inasmuch as ye did it not to one of the least of these, ye did it not to me.

46 And these shall go away into everlasting punishment: but the righteous unto life eternal.

You do not need to know someone before you show

kindness. Although it is recommended for you to make an impact on your world, you were not blessed for your own benefit alone, but to be a solution unto others. It does not matter what their culture, gender, creed, religion etc are. Remember the story of the Good Samaritan. He never knew the man that was attacked and wounded by thieves but in an act of passion, he believed that he was a human being like him, with no prejudice, no racial discrimination or creed, so he came to rescue him. Jesus declared that as soon as you show your love towards one another, it is good to fast and pray, but the right discipline for effective results is for you to abide towards God's commandments, loving and live in holiness and righteousness. This will enable the ultimate way forward towards the narrow road that leads to Heaven.

We are God's creations and He is a universal God. If the Almighty God could spare His only begotten Son for sacrificial offering. Brethren, what is within your reach that you can utilize to influence people around you? A little grocery shopping, a few minutes of phone calls to seek for their well-being, just to say hello. It may be nothing to you, but it might be very significant and precious to another fellow in need. All this is accredited towards the Heavenly Kingdom through the strait gate.

Chapter Three

FASTING AND PRAYERS

As stated, prayer is the key to breakthrough, and Jesus is our role model to emulate for the accepted way of life (Jeremiah 29: 12-13):

12 Then shall ye call upon me, and ye shall go and pray unto me, and I will hearken unto you.

13 And ye shall seek me, and find me, when ye shall search for me with all your heart.

Let us reflect on the scenario of a man negatively referred to as Jabez. It might be due to parental circumstances or because of his family background that his mother named him after sorrow (1st Chronicles 4:9-10):

9 And Jabez was more honourable than his brethren: and his mother called his name Jabez, saying, Because I bare him with sorrow.

10 And Jabez called on the God of Israel, saying, Oh that thou wouldest bless me indeed, and enlarge my coast, and that thine hand might be with me, and that thou wouldest keep me from evil, that it may not grieve me! And God granted him that which he requested.

Jabez made a plea to God in prayer, and tabled all his requests signified in Verse 10. All requests were granted, and a negative parental proclamation was turned into an accomplishment that contradicted his foundation. You can turn that ugly situation round when you raise a holy lamentation towards Heaven. Do not forget that many times a prophecy would be pronounced but the manifestation depends on individual responsibility. If you take that bold step as a child of God, table it to Him in prayer, then surely He will answer (Matthew 11:12):

And from the days of John the Baptist until now the Kingdom of Heaven suffereth violence, and the violent take it by force.

Saints, if there is no contention, there is no possession. Any good gift can only be obtained with potency. Your dream can only come to realisation with the power of God raised in prayer and fasting. The accuser of the brethren is out there awaiting your downfall, but by the special grace of God they will wait forever. You and I shall never fall nor fail. Prayer is a means of communication to Our Father for worshipping and honouring Him. Even, from the account of Daniel, after several days of fasting and prayers with no signs he was visited by Michael the archangel, who reassured him that God had answered his supplication.

Daniel 10:10-14:

10 And behold, a hand touched me, which set me upon my knees and upon the palms of my hands.

11 And he said unto me, O Daniel, a man greatly beloved, understand the words that I speak unto thee, and stand upright: for unto thee am I now sent. And when he had spoken this word unto me, I stood trembling.

12 Then said he unto me, Fear not, Daniel: for from the first day that thou didst set thine heart to understand, and to chasten thyself before thy God, thy words were heard, and I am come for thy words.

13 But the prince of the Kingdom of Persia withstood me one and twenty days: but, lo, Michael, one of the chief princes, came to help me; and I remained there with the kings of Persia.

14 Now I am come to make thee understand what shall befall thy people in the latter days: for yet the vision is for many days.

Daniel was told that the very first day he commenced his request unto God, all was granted, but the devil hindered the prayer, the prince of

Persia, the principalities and powers, the rulers of darkness. To be victorious all you need is to execute supplications on your knees in prayers with fasting. Therefore, we should be aware that God continually reigns in the affairs of men, but you have to persevere, by keeping on praying until good results happen. Prayer is a command from God, and you cannot obtain anything without asking Him. He never fails! He is the one of yesterday, today and forever. He changes not.

Jesus' whole lifestyle was passionately sold into prayer. He could not have functioned effectively without fasting and prayer. He taught His disciples how to pray without ceasing (Matthew 6: 5-15):

5 *And when thou prayest, thou shalt not be as the hypocrites are: for they love to pray standing in the synagogues and in the corners of the streets, that they may be seen of men. Verily I say unto you, They have their reward.*

6 *But thou, when thou prayest, enter into thy closet, and when thou hast shut thy door, pray to thy Father which is in*

secret; and thy Father which is in secret; and thy Father which seeth in secret shall reward thee openly.

7 *But when ye pray, use not vain repetitions, as the heathen do: for they think that they shall be heard for their much speaking.*

8 *Be not ye therefore like unto them: for your Father knoweth what things ye have need of before ye ask him.*

9 *After this manner therefore pray ye: Our Father which art in Heaven, Hallowed be thy name.*

10 *Thy Kingdom come. Thy will be done in earth, as it is in Heaven.*

11 *Give us this day our daily bread.*

12 *And forgive us our debts, as we forgive our debtors.*

13 *And lead us not into temptation, but deliver us from evil: For thine is the Kingdom, and the power, and the glory, for ever Amen.*

14 For if ye forgive men their trespasses, your Heavenly Father will also forgive you.

15 But if ye forgive not men their trespasses, neither will your Father forgive your trespasses.

The Lord is demonstrating to us that praying, fasting and giving of alms is unto Him our Creator, not unto any carnal man. It is an indication that Jesus noticed the attitude of some people towards giving an offering during service. Jesus knows the intention of everyone. People attend services with diverse motives. Some want to be noticed showing their wealth via their offering or admired for their latest attire, thereby intimidating the poor among the congregation. There are some people who fail to attend Sunday services just because they feel excluded for not being up to the dress standard. They don't belong to a social group. To avoid distraction, a good Christian is permitted to dress well but decently.

No wonder Jesus Christ was able to identify the widow's mite. She brought all that she had from the heart of thanksgiving, and in appreciation, the offering was accepted. While glamorous men and women come in with their regalia displaying their offerings, the owner of the church X-rays individual hearts, and is able to identify who is genuinely offering gifts unto God.

However, giving an offering is an act of worshipping God where your left hand should not know what the right hand is offering. You give willingly, and this is between you and God, who is a rewarder. After praying and fasting, the Lord made it a requirement to offer unto those that have nothing, or who cannot afford to give. Thereby as you do this, you are giving unto the Lord. God is sending you to be a solution, a problem solver to someone, an angel on God's assignment for the poor. Thereafter, when you call, instantly He will answer.

So also, Jesus Christ agonised in prayer in the garden of Gethsemane before he was nailed to the cross for our redemption (Matthew 26:36-44):

36 Then cometh Jesus with them unto a place called Gethsemane, and saith unto the disciples, Sit ye here, while I go and pray yonder.

37 And he took with him Peter and the two sons of Zebedee, and began to be sorrowful and very heavy.

38 Then said he unto them, My soul is exceeding sorrowful, even unto death: tarry ye here, and watch with me.

39 And he went a little farther, and fell on his face, and prayed, saying, O my Father, if it be possible, let this cup pass from me: nevertheless not as I will, but as thou will.

40 And he cometh unto the disciples, and findeth them asleep, and saith unto Peter, What, could ye not watch with me one hour?

41 Watch and pray, that ye enter not into temptation: the spirit indeed is willing, but the flesh is weak.

42 He went away again the second time, and prayed, saying, O my Father, if this cup may not pass away from me, except I drink it, thy will be done.

43 And he came and found them asleep again for their eyes were heavy.

44 And he left them, and went away again, and prayed the third time, saying the same words.

45 Then cometh he to his disciples, and saith unto them, Sleep on now, and take your rest: behold, the hour is at hand, and the Son of man is betrayed into the hands of sinners.

46 Rise, let us be going: behold, he is at hand that doth betray me.

Jesus was around the Mount of Olives for solitude, but He went with some of the inner group from His disciples for prayers, namely Peter, James and John. His prayer point was for the cup to pass over Him, not because He was scared of death, but solely in obedience to His Father's will. Hence the sinless Christ dies for the sin of the world. In various instances there will always be someone assigned by God to share the word of encouragement when you are going through challenges. When trials come, you only look unto God the author and finisher of your faith. Thus the wilderness experiences of life are between you and your God. Christianity is a personal relationship with your Father and if there is no pain there will never be gain. Jesus went through trials, and He passed them successfully. To name but a few in the Bible, Job, Abraham, Joseph, David and Queen Esther passed the test of life. You and I shall also triumph over every trial of life in Jesus' name.

So also, prayer can move mountains, as indicated during an incident when the disciples found it provoking for the healing of a boy possessed with an evil spirit (Matthew 17: 14-21):

14 And when they were come to the multitude, there came to him a certain man, kneeling down to him, and saying.

15 Lord, have mercy on my son: for he is lunatic, and sore vexed: for ofttimes he falleth into the fire, and oft into the water.

16 And I brought him to thy disciples, and they could not cure him.

17 Then Jesus answered and said, O faithless and perverse generation, how long shall I be with you? How long shall I suffer you? bring him hither to me.

18 And Jesus rebuked the devil; and he departed out of him: and the child was cured from that very hour.

19 Then came the disciples to Jesus apart, and said, Why could not we cast him out?

20 And Jesus said unto them, Because of your unbelief: for verily I say unto you, If ye have faith as a grain of mustard seed, ye shall say unto this mountain, Remove hence to yonder place; and it shall remove; and nothing shall be impossible unto you.

21 Howbeit this kind goeth not out but by prayer and fasting.

The disciple of Christ made an effort to cure the boy that was brought with a lunatic illness, but due to their unbelief they were unable to heal him. Jesus categorically declared that without faith and assurance in God, it is impossible to have a positive outcome. Hence, miracles can only manifest through fasting and prayers as you believe it is a standard for fulfilment. A prayerless

Christian is a powerless believer. It is through prayers that believers are strengthened and empowered during difficult times, for He is always with you and will never leave you alone nor forsake you.

Nonetheless, Jesus was strengthened by an angel while in agony at the garden of Gethsemane before he was crucified. He started with prayer and ended with prayer; that is the key to breakthrough. Despite all the agony, Jesus prayed and interceded for His accusers on the cross while he stated in Luke 23:34:

Then said Jesus, Father, forgive them; for they know not what they do. And they parted His raiment, and cast lots.

So also, the manifestations of the effectiveness of prayer was when Job prayed for his friends and all that he lost was restored (Job 42:10):

And the LORD turned the captivity of Job, when he prayed for his friends: also the Lord gave Job twice as much as he had before.

Job interceded for his associates, as the Lord

expected believers to do likewise. When you determine to seek the wellbeing of others, God will raise help for your needs. When you pray, the Lord will grant all your petitions. The Kingdom race is personal. There are times when you have to separate yourself and reverence God in solitude, just to be alone with God. Prayer is the key to success, both spiritually and from the secular point of view. Be able to discipline yourself by living a holy, and righteous lifestyle, incubated in prayer and fasting without ceasing, for the Kingdom of Heaven's sake.

For prayers to be effectively answered you must ensure that you held no man any grudges. Hence, the heart of forgiveness is a compulsory principle towards eternity.

Chapter Four

FORGIVENESS

The Lord emphasised from the account of Matthew 6:12 that before you offer anything unto God, if anyone has hurt you, you have no choice other than to forgive and let go before giving offering on the altar of God. Saints, this is the Kingdom principle. If you refuse to forgive and let go, another person somewhere will be holding you too. Therefore, forgiveness is very important towards Heavenly mandate. It could be very painful if someone has really wronged you, but obedience is the criterion to access that eternal life.

From the account of Matthew 18:21-35, Jesus expressed concerns on forgiveness:

21 Then came Peter to him, and said, Lord, how oft shall my brother sin against me, and I forgive him? till seven times?

22 Jesus saith unto him, I say not unto thee, Until seven times: but, Until seventy times seven.

23 Therefore is the Kingdom of Heaven likened unto a certain king, which would take account of his servants.

24 And when he had begun to reckon, one was brought unto him, which owned him ten thousand talents.

25 But forasmuch as he had not to pay, his lord commanded him to be sold, and his wife, and children, and all that he had, and payment to be made.

26 The servant therefore fell down, and worshiped him, saying, Lord, have patience with me, and I will pay thee all.

27 Then the lord of that servant was moved with compassion, and loosed him, and forgave him the debt.

28 But the same servant went out, and found one of his fellow servants, which owned him a hundred pence: and he laid hands on him, and took him by the throat, saying, Pay me that thou owest.

29 And his fellow servant fell down at his feet, and besought him, saying, Have patience with me, and I will pay thee all.

30 And he would not: but went and cast him into prison, till he should pay the debt.

31 So when his fellow servants saw what was done, they were very sorry, and came and told unto their lord all that was done.

32 Then his lord, after that he had called him, said unto him, O thou wicked servant, I forgave thee all that debt, because thou desiredst me:

33 Shouldest not thou also have had compassion on thy fellow servant, even as I had pity on thee?

34 And his lord was wroth, and delivered him to the tormentors, till he should pay all that was due unto him.

35 So likewise shall my Heavenly Father do also unto you, if ye from your hearts forgive not everyone his brother their trespasses.

The above verses with regard to forgiveness make it look as if it was irresistible to the disciples who encouraged Peter to enquire how a brother/sister could sin and be forgiven seven times, but Jesus responded, not only seven but seven multiplied by seventy. Thus, uncountable and indefinite times of forgiveness will portray a real follower of Christ. Jesus describes in His parables how the unforgiving servant was supposed to have supported other brethren that owned him, but forgetting is by God's sovereign power, and the value of being compassionate to others is that he got his freedom through forgiveness. Therefore,

Jesus illustrated the fact that believers who have been forgiven excessively by God are never to refuse forgiveness from others, who must have owed for some reasonable immaterial offence.

The Lord's demonstration of love is that believers are one family; if you have been betrayed, hurts and sins must have encroached you, but He is advising us to go all the way for reconciliation, to reunite and sort out all differences. Hence, forgiveness is to be utilised frequently, because it is an essential tool to heal every wound, for narrow is that path to the Heavenly Kingdom.

Brethren, rest assured that whatever challenge you may have been through, it would not take long for a supernatural turning around. The Lord is saying to you and me, do not give up! Though it may have been delayed, it is not denied. Wait and see the salvation of God. He is able.

Another criterion that enables access towards the strait route is humility, thus the death of the flesh.

Chapter Five

SUBDUE THE FLESH

The flesh must die to create the Heavenly alliance with God which is the sole pathway towards the everlasting life. Two cannot work together without coming to a convincing agreement (Amos 3:3). You can only achieve that by living a life that pleases God. The spirit and flesh do wrestle together, but you must discipline yourself. A sinful nature might be tempting, by acting negatively, but the Holy Spirit will rebuke it; take it and nail it to the cross with faith. Envy, jealousy, unforgiveness, backbiting, hypocrisy, idolatry etc are of the flesh. You make a demand

and tell God in prayers and fasting that will enable you to crucify flesh in order to eradicate every ill thought for the accomplishment of the Kingdom of Heaven.

According to the following Scriptures stated in the book of Galatians 5:16-26:

16 This I say then, Walk in the Spirit, and ye shall not fulfil the lust of the flesh.

17 For the flesh lusteth against the Spirit, and the Spirit against the flesh: and these are contrary the one to the other: so that ye cannot do the things that ye would.

18 But if ye be led of the Spirit, ye are not under the law.

19 Now the works of the flesh are manifest, which are these: adultery, fornication, uncleanness, lasciviousness,

20 Idolatry, witchcraft, hatred, variance, emulations, wrath, strife, seditions, heresies,

21 Envyings, murders, drunkenness, revellings, and such like: of which I tell you before, as I have also told you in time past, that they which do such things shall not inherit the Kingdom of God.

22 But the fruit of the Spirit is love, joy, peace, long-sufferings, gentleness, goodness, faith.

23 Meekness, temperance: against such there is no law.

24 And they that are Christ's have crucified the flesh with the affections and lusts.

26 If we live in the Spirit, let us also walk in the Spirit.

26 Let us not be desirous of vain glory, provoking one another, envying one another.

Consider the believer's freedom in Christ, which is for us to live by faith so that we enable ourselves to be new creatures in Him. The newness is never found by indulging desires of a sinful nature, but rather in loving. The law will demonstrate how love should be executed, but the law never generates any affection from your mind, while the Holy Spirit is unyielding to any immoral desires. Rather, the Spirit will yield fruit in human nature in comparison to the ambiguous products of wickedness. Also, the Spirit of the living God produces the love, joy, peace, patience, kindness, goodness, faithfulness, gentleness and self-discipline that men always strive to achieve. However, in some instances they could not accomplish this, except by having a close relationship with Him. Doubtless, the law contradicts the realm of the Holy Ghost which is by no means beneficial to humanity. Therefore, it is recommended to obey His commandments and engage in things of God, showing love and living a lifestyle for the approved pathway.

Christianity never centres on rules but on relationships. The ultimate goal is to love God, as He first loved the human race. The Lord is making a demand for His followers to work out their salvation with fear and trembling, because God did not spare His only begotten Son, so we have to walk in accordance with His precepts (Matthew 27:46):

And about the ninth hour Jesus cried with a loud voice, saying Eli, Eli, Lama sabachthani? that is to say, MY GOD, MY GOD, WHY HAST THOU FORSAKEN ME?

The Saviour of humanity, who was sinless, cried in agony as a price paid for atonement. Therefore, walking in the Spirit, Christians must believe that the Spirit is embedded inside the individual, and only depends on the Holy Spirit for assistance during it's the time of need. It is for empowering the saints, in as much as they abide to His laid-down values and live lifestyles pleasing unto God. It is advisable for believers to be aware that though we live in the world, we should not be carried away by materialism, but engaged in a disciplined way of life in order to subdue the flesh. To be disciplined is to honour and fear God, and to be accountable for fulfilment. However, the arm of flesh will fail you because the best of men are still man. God is sovereign and just as He declared in (Jeremiah 17:5):

Thus saith the LORD; Cursed be the man that trusteth in man and maketh flesh his arm, and whose heart departeth from the LORD.

There was an incident of King Saul trying to please flesh, and he could be referred to as a men pleaser (1st Samuel 15:24-30):

24 And Saul said unto Samuel, I have sinned: for I have transgressed the commandment of the LORD, and thy words: because I feared the people, and obeyed their voice.

25 Now therefore, I pray thee, pardon my sin, and turn again with me, that I may worship the LORD.

26 And Samuel said unto Saul, I will not return with thee: for thou hast rejected the word of the LORD, and the LORD hath rejected thee from being king over Israel.

27 And as Samuel turned about to go away, he laid hold upon the skirt of his mantle, and it rent.

28 And Samuel said unto him, The LORD hath rent the Kingdom of Israel from thee this day, and hath given it to a neighbour of thine, that is better than thou.

29 And also the Strength of Israel will not lie nor repent: for he is not a man, that he should repent.

30 Then he said, I have sinned: yet honour me now, I pray thee, before the elders of my people, and before Israel, and turn again with me, that I may worship the LORD thy God.

The natural man cannot go through the confined way. Hence, one needs to be born again, to be redeemed through the Blood of Jesus Christ, able to subdue the flesh before you can obtain access to the constricted route. Those who are living unrighteous lifestyles cannot obtain this access, as they were dominated by sin. The above stanzas narrated how King Saul could not adhere to the voice of God through His prophet but rather yielded to people's opinions. Hence the verses were indicating to everyone the supremacy and authenticity of the only Sovereign God towards a perfect end. For example, when a seed is planted in the soil, after a few months it will grow, reproducing much more than just a single seed, and so also the aftermath when you die to self thus: to subdue the flesh. You advertise Christ through your way of life. People would like to emulate and relate to you, doing the will of God in obedience to His commandment as rightly stated in the ten commandments embedded in the Love of Christ. King Saul never realised that no man created by God is indispensable. This event is for our learning, and for the saints of God not to fall into the same faults.

God has given the individual an assignment. It is for you to pray, to recognise the plan and purpose of God for your life. You can never be fulfilled where you were not called to be, but rather pray for His direction. Saul got it wrong when he was trying to officiate the priestly role that was not meant for him. No wonder! There are many false prophets out there using the name of God for materialism. It is high time you changed, except you were called. It is the instruction released to you by God that you will be accountable for. May the Almighty count you and me worthy at the end of this Christianity race, because this is a sensitive path that all creatures of God have to be very cautious about your role of assignment that will not hinder entry to the everlasting Kingdom.

The Lord is the owner of Heaven and earth, and whether you are operating within the secular or the spiritual realm, God is the controller. He monitors your doings, so let's strive to obey His commandment. Whatever you have been through, or whatever challenges you undergo, be encouraged and have assurance that you are not alone. He makes all things beautiful in His own time as declared in Luke 1:37: ***For with God nothing shall be impossible***.

There is a description of God's sovereignty in the book of Joshua, and how he was reassured by God after the death of Moses his master. As a result, we all need encouragement from God and man.

Chapter Six

ENCOURAGEMENT

The Lord can screen you from the inside out to expose any concealed issues. Therefore, He was able to assess Joshua, as He demonstrated to him that so far he could keep and abide to His Commandments He would guide him all through; as He walked with Moses his master, He would do the same. What an encouragement! The fear of the Lord is almost lost universally in this age of scientific development because, if people feared God, they would guide against a sinful way of life, avoiding double standards of living etc. You cannot compromise with sin and still claim to be on the Lord's side. Nonetheless, as the Lord reassured His servant (Joshua), the same is applicable to believers of this time in the book of Joshua 1:1-9:

1   Now after the death of Moses the servant of the LORD it came to pass, that the LORD spake unto Joshua the son of Nun, Moses minister, saying,

2   Moses my servant is dead; now therefore arise, go over this Jordan, thou, and all this people, unto the land which I do give to them, even to the children of Israel.

3   Every place that the sole of your foot shall tread upon, that have I given unto you, as I said unto Moses.

4   From the wilderness and this Lebanon even unto the great river, the river Euphrates, all the land of the Hittites, and unto the Great Sea toward the going down of the sun, shall be your coast.

5 There shall not any man be able to stand before thee all the days of thy life: as I was with Moses, so I will be with thee: I will not fail thee, nor forsake thee.

6 Be strong and of a good courage: for unto this people shalt thou divide for an inheritance the land, which I sware unto their fathers to give them.

7 Only be thou strong and very courageous, that thou mayest observe to do according to all the law, which Moses my servant commanded thee: turn not from it to the right hand or to the left, that thou mayest prosper whithersoever thou goest.

8 This book of the law shall not depart out of thy mouth; but thou shalt meditate therein day and night, that thou mayest observe to do according to all that is written therein: for then thou shalt make thy way prosperous, and then thou shalt have good success.

9   *Have not I commanded thee? Be strong and of a good courage; be not afraid, neither be thou dismayed: for the LORD thy God is with thee whithersoever thou goest.*

From verses 6-9, repeated word of encouragement from God reassured Joshua not to be afraid, but to be encouraged and be bold, strong that He will always be leading him through. The LORD is reassuring you to be encouraged, and to forge ahead. Take a bold step of faith and march forward to execute that vision or project, that career, or whatever God has commanded or laid into your heart towards the Kingdom for fulfilment. Do not look at the faces of people that surround you, or any form of distraction or discouragement, even fear of failing. Whenever you fail, it doesn't mean that you are a failure, it is experiential: a learning process, thereby gaining you experience.

Saints, be aware that fear is the greatest obstacle to the plan and purpose of God. Therefore, be courageous and fear not! Fear and doubt are the opposite of faith, which is the enemy of breakthrough and the vital devices behind the purposeful achievements, visions, dreams and fulfilment in life. Even before you were born, your Creator knew you from your mother's womb. You have been anointed right from your mother's womb. Jesus made that declaration (Jeremiah 1:4-19) but from verses 4-11 and 17-19:

4 Then the word of the Lord came unto me, saying,

5 Before I formed thee in the belly I knew thee; and before thou camest forth out of the womb I sanctified thee, and I ordained thee a prophet unto the nations.

6 Then said I, Ah, Lord GOD! Behold I cannot speak: for I am a child.

7 But the LORD said unto me, Say not, I am a child: for thou shalt go to all that I shall send thee, and whatsoever I command thee thou shalt speak.

8 Be not afraid of their faces: for I am with thee to deliver thee, saith the LORD.

9 Then the LORD put forth his hand, and touched my mouth. And the LORD said unto me, Behold, I have put my words in thy mouth.

10 See, I have this day set thee over the nations and over the Kingdoms, to root out, and to pull down, and to destroy, and to throw down, to build, and to plant.

11 Moreover the word of the LORD came unto me, saying, Jeremiah, what seest thou? And I said, I see a rod of an almond tree.

Emphasis is laid on encouragement and reassurance from the Lord unto Jeremiah not to be afraid nor dismayed, that HE was with him, as he obeyed the commandment and abided by the will of God. The Lord is ministering to you and me also that we should not be afraid, because fear is the strategy of the devil. So also, from verses 17-19:

17 Thou therefore gird up thy loins, and arise, and speak unto them all that I command thee: be not dismayed at their faces, lest I confound thee before them.

18 For, behold, I have made thee this day a defensed city; and an iron pillar, and brazen walls against the whole land, against the kings of Judah, against the princes thereof, against the priests thereof, and against the people of the land.

19 And they shall fight against thee; but they shall not prevail against thee; for I am with thee, saith the LORD, to deliver thee.

Verse 18 signifies that Jehovah is our defence and further stresses that no matter the devices of the enemies, He the Almighty God will surely deliver His people. The Lord is addressing His saints at this period and saying that as you obey, believe that He is able to do exceedingly, abundantly without hesitation. All you need to do is obey according to His will while victory is sure.

Let us deliberate on the account of how Queen Esther, with no quality background, became a renowned personality. She was replaced, while Vashti was displaced due to pride and disobedience.

May we not be displaced from the plan and purpose of God in Jesus' Name Amen. Queen Esther delivered her people from bondage because of humility and obedience to her uncle Mordecai. According to Esther 4:8-9, 14-17:

8 Also he gave him the copy of the writing of the decree that was given at Shushan to destroy them, to show it unto Esther, and to declare it unto her, and to charge her that she should go in unto the king, to make supplication unto him, and to make request before him for her people.

9 And Hatach came and told Esther the words of Mordecai.

10 For if thou altogether holdest thy peace at this time, then shall there enlargement and deliverance arise to the Jews from another place; but thou and thy father's house shall be destroyed: and who knoweth whether thou art come to the Kingdom for such a time as this?

11 Then Esther bade them return Mordecai this answer,

12 Go, gather together all the Jews that are present in Shushan, and fast ye for me, and neither eat nor drink three days, night or day: I also and my maidens will fast likewise; and so will I go in unto the king, which is not according to the law: and if I perish, I perish.

13 So Mordecai went his way, and did according to all that Esther had commanded him.

Queen Esther was a risk taker, and business is a risk. The Lord inspires believers to be bold, courageous in others to accomplish that ultimate goal, either, career wise, ministerial, or in business etc, for fulfilment. Practically, I suggest you should be always alert, in readiness, taking action in the right place and at the appropriate time. Jesus Christ was an action man, moving with signs, always doing wonders and focusing on His Father's business.

This takes us to the next feature of treading the strait gate, as it were, in Ephesians 5:9:

(For the fruit of the Spirit is in all goodness and righteousness and truth;)

Apostle Paul laid emphasis that believers should make every effort to be filled with the Spirit of God and live in holiness; this is very important as we represent Jesus. We are created in the likeness of God, so we try as much as possible to do the right thing at the appropriate time. We are the ambassadors of Christ, hence our lives should specify the goodness and righteousness and be empowered to be speaking the undiluted word of truth, thus taking prompt action, avoiding procrastination and negative perception/doubt and being slothful in professional goals, even things of God. No one can access the narrow gate as a sluggish follower of Christ.

Chapter Seven

SLOTHFULNESS

By the power of the Holy Spirit for us to walk in the path of righteousness, be aware that a slothful man cannot attain any reward. Proverbs 26: 13-28:

13 The slothful man saith, There is a lion in the way; a lion is in the streets.

14 As the door turneth upon his hinges, so doth the slothful upon his bed.

15 The slothful hideth his hand in his boson; it grieveth him to bring it again to his mouth.

16 The sluggard is wiser in his own conceit than seven men that can render a reason.

17 He that passeth by, and meddleth with strife belonging not to him, is like one that taketh a dog by the ears.

18 As a mad man who casteth firebrands, arrows, and death,

19 So is the man that deceiveth his neighbour, and saith, Am not I in sport?

20 Where no wood is, there the fire goeth out: so where there is no talebearer, the strife ceaseth.

21 As coals are to burning coals, and wood to fire; so is a contentions man to kindle strife.

22 The words of a talebearer are as wounds, and they go down into the innermost parts of the belly.

23 Burning lips and a wicked heart are like a potsherd covered with silver dross.

24 He that hateth dissembleth with his lips, and layeth up deceit within him,

25 When he speaketh fair, believe him not: for there are seven abominations in his heart.

26 Whose hatred is covered by deceit, his wickedness shall be showed before the whole congregation.

27 Whoso diggeth a pit shall fall therein: and he that rolleth a stone, it will return upon him.

28 A lying tongue hateth those that are afflicted by it; and a flattering mouth worketh ruin.

The slothful person loves to sleep, to the extent that he/she loves to stay in bed, giving irrelevant excuses. A slothful being must have been given an assignment, but due to negative personality and bad attitude that does not conform to biblical principles, unable to execute any project. Therefore, with the habits of going about gossiping, he/she becomes a tale bearer presenting him/herself as a community informant, instead of minding the business God has assigned for his/her destiny. Saints of God should be careful, because words are powerful, you never know where people are coming from, what challenges they must have been through in life, or their relationship with God. Whosoever is tearing others down with that little object (the tongue), the sword which is meant for prayers, except repentance, as stated in the word of God, anyone with such negative characteristics will be deprived of accessing the narrow gate that leads towards God's Kingdom. Hence, it is never too late to deviate from malpractice. On the contrary, faith without work is deadly. Therefore, to be active is healthy to the body, soul and spirit in accordance with James 2:17: ***Even so faith, if it hath not works, is dead, being alone.***

The question is, if God has given you promises and you are expecting Him to fulfil them, you must take a bold step of faith and try to embark on something. Do your bit, then God will do the rest by enhancing it.

What steps have you taken to make that expectation of yours become a reality? Taking no action will be an abomination to God's promises. Although God must have pronounced or made a declaration, your intention and motives will allow the power of the Holy Spirit to energise and bring it to pass, but not by folding your arms or giving excuses such as lack of education, family background, your past history, or saying you have tried but yielded no positive outcomes, or due to past failure. Beloved, rest assured that God is in the midst of that situation, and never give up on your dream, that vision, goal, project etc. God will test your faith; it is only with your move or when you take that courageous step that the Almighty God will back you up for its manifestation.

The Shunammite woman observed that Prophet Elisha as he always passes through their thoroughfare was a man of God (2nd Kings 4:8-17):

8 And it fell on a day, that Elisha passed to Shunem, where was a great woman; and she constrained him to eat bread. And so it was, that as oft as he passed by, he turned in thither to eat bread.

9 And she said unto her husband, Behold now, I perceive that this is a holy man of God, which passeth by us continually.

10 Let us make a little chamber, I pray thee, on the wall; and let us set for him there a bed, and a table, and a stool, and a candlestick: and it shall be, when he cometh to us, that he shall turn in thither.

11 *And it fell on a day, that he came thither, and he turned into the chamber, and lay there.*

12 *And he said to Gehazi his servant, Call this Shunammite. And when he had called her, she stood before him.*

13 *And he said unto him, Say now unto her, Behold, thou hast been careful for us with all this care; what is to be done for thee? Wouldest thou be spoken for to the king, or to the captain of the host? And she answered, I dwell among mine own people.*

14 *And he said, What then is to be done for her? And Gehazi answered, Verily she hath no child, and her husband is old.*

15 *And he said, Call her. And when he had called her, she stood in the door.*

16 *And he said, About this season, according to the time of life, thou shalt embrace a son. And she said, Nay, my*

lord, thou man of God, do not lie unto thine handmaid.

17 And the woman conceived, and bare a son at that season that Elisha had said unto her, according to the time of life.

This woman was moved, very passionate, charitable and able to entertain guests: she ministered to men of God. She perceived, by the power of the Holy Spirit that was embedded in her, after waiting for quite a long period trusting God for the fruit of the womb, there was no positive fruitfulness. She took it on board to aid the work of God in faith, not by folding her arms but embarking on doing good within her environment. She took a bold step of faith after seeking the consent of the husband, as they both believed in God. She provoked the move of God. However, this was contrary to some spouses, who would instantly refuse to let in strangers to their homes, or even allow the entertainment of guests. Whatever good deeds you must have done, you are sowing towards the internal rewards for your future. Unknowingly some faithful servants of God have entertained angels that resulted in a turning point: their season of laughter. May your miracles come quickly too. The event whereby Abraham and Sarah were blessed with the son of promise, Genesis 18:1-15:

1 And the LORD appeared unto him in the plains of Mamre: and he sat in the tent door in the heat of the day.

2 And he lifted up his eyes and looked, and, lo, three men stood by him: and when he saw them, he ran to meet them from the tent door, and bowed himself toward the ground,

3 And said, My Lord, if now I have found favour in thy sight, pass not away, I pray thee, from thy servant:

4 Let a little water, I pray you, be fetched, and wash your feet, and rest yourselves under the tree:

5 And I will fetch a morsel of bread, and comfort ye your hearts; after that ye shall pass on: for therefore are ye come to your servant. And they said, So do, as thou hast said.

6 *And Abraham hastened into the tent unto Sarah, and said, Make ready quickly three measures of fine meal, knead it, and make cakes upon the hearth.*

7 *And Abraham ran unto the herd, and fetched a calf tender and good, and gave it unto a young man; and he hasted to dress it.*

8 *And he took butter, and milk, and the calf which he had dressed, and set it before them; and he stood by them under the tree, and they did eat.*

9 *And they said unto him, Where is Sarah thy wife? And he said, Behold, in the tent.*

10 *And he said, I will certainly return unto thee according to the time of life; and, lo, Sarah thy wife shall have a son. And Sarah heard it in the tent door, which was behind him.*

11 *Now Abraham and Sarah were old and well stricken in age; and it ceased to be with Sarah after the manner of women.*

12 Therefore Sarah laughed within herself, saying, After I am waxed old shall I have pleasure, my lord being old also?

13 And the LORD said unto Abraham, Wherefore did Sarah laugh, saying, Shall I of a surety bear a child, which am old?

14 Is anything too hard for the LORD? At the time appointed I will return unto thee, according to the time of life, and Sarah shall have a son.

15 Then Sarah denied, saying, I laughed not; for she was afraid. And he said, Nay: but thou didst laugh.

Abraham was a man of faith, sensitive by the power of the Holy Spirit.

God is a Spirit: and they that worship him must worship him in spirit and in truth (John 4:24).

Abraham was able to acknowledge that the guests were not ordinary beings (Genesis 18: Verses 2). He worshipped and reverenced God in their lives while he never knew that Yahweh

Himself was among the two angels. He entertained angels unawares because he could perceive from the spirit. Being a man with liberal way of life, he actively participated in the preparation of the food, but Abraham took action, not being sluggish nor slothful, as he quickly made arrangements to make his guests comfortable. Even Sarah, his wife, corporately embraced their master's visitors (Verse 4). Within a twinkling of an eye, he passed instruction and prepared food (Verses 6-8). After undergoing this process of entertainment, so also, the washing of their feet was a cultural norm. Jesus Christ laid an example for us to emulate (John 13: 5):

After that he poureth water into a basin, and began to wash the disciples' feet, and to wipe them with the towel wherewith he was girded.

Jesus was not being slothful, abled to washed His disciples' feet indicates an evident of a good leader, in humility and act of service. Though, it was supposed to be the other way round but to show a positive and good model for us to follow.

Nevertheless, Abraham and his household

were engaged in the cleaning, cooking and making of a big dinner, never an easy task. There was no notification about these guests, whom they never expected. If he was lazy or slothful, he would have missed that golden opportunity. Even in our generation, before a guest is invited there must be notification due to busy schedules. Abraham never knew how God would fulfil His promise. Surprisingly, it was after the meal that the angels made that declaration (Verses 10) and the long-awaited promise of God, when all hope was lost, came to pass.

Yahweh fulfilled His promise and reaffirmed there was nothing too difficult for the Lord God to handle (Verse 14). Abraham passed this test because of his faith in whom he believed; and he was actively involved due to his lifestyle of hospitality. The question is: are you and I passion about the things of God? If not, it is time to arise and emulate Christ, in doing good that leads to Heaven via the narrow access of excellence performance.

Additionally, the episode that took place at the pool of Bethesda (John 5:1-16):

1 *After this there was a feast of the Jews; and Jesus went up to Jerusalem.*

2 *Now there is at Jerusalem by the sheep market a pool, which is called in the Hebrew tongue Bethesda, having five porches.*

3 *In these lay a great multitude of impotent folk, of blind, halt, withered, waiting for the moving of the water.*

4 *For an angel went down at a certain season into the pool, and troubled the water: whosoever then first after the troubling of the water stepped in was made whole of whatsoever disease he had.*

5 *And a certain man was there, which had an infirmity thirty and eight years.*

6 *When Jesus saw him lie, and knew that he had been now a long time in that case, he saith unto him, Wilt thou be made whole?*

7 *The impotent man answered him, Sir, I have no man, when the water is troubled, to put me into the pool: but*

while I am coming, another steppeth down before me.

8 *Jesus saith unto him, Rise, take up thy bed, and walk.*

9 *And immediately the man was made whole, and took up his bed, and walked: and on the same day was the Sabbath.*

10 *The Jews therefore said unto him that was cured, It is the Sabbath day: it is not lawful for thee to carry thy bed.*

11 *He answered them, He that made me whole, the same said unto me, Take up thy bed, and walk.*

12 *Then asked they him, What man is that which said unto thee, Take up thy bed, and walk?*

13 *And he that was healed wist not who it was: for Jesus had conveyed himself away, a multitude being in that place.*

14 *Afterward Jesus findeth him in the temple, and said unto him, Behold, thou art made whole: sin no more, lest a worse thing come unto thee.*

15 The man departed, and told the Jews that it was Jesus, which had made him whole.

16 And therefore did the Jews persecute Jesus, and sought to slay him, because he had done these things on the Sabbath day.

This Pool of Bethesda was connected by five porticos which would have been difficult for the lame man to pass through. Due to his faith and not being slothful, but zealously awaiting help, after seeing Jesus he was still expressing how he had been trying for quite a long time before the birth of Jesus, trusting God for Mercy as (Bethesda) meaning the House of Mercy. That is how some brethren are going through the challenges of life; you just have to believe in Him, persevere, trusting Him and hoping prayerfully that one day Jesus will step into that situation.

As the Lord stepped into this man's case, He will step into any issues of life that are questioning the authority of God in your life in Jesus' name Amen.

Do you realise that when people are faced with

challenges, you are in most cases by yourself, because there is no one except God? This lame man was dropped by family or friends, always left alone until Jesus divinely interceded.

Be rest assured that Jehovah Emmanuel is always with us. He never fails! Jesus Christ the same yesterday, and today, and for ever (Hebrews 13:8).

Reflecting (verses 10-12), when some of the Jews inquired from this man, there arose controversial issues against the law that forbade anything to be done on the Sabbath day. People have forgotten that this man had been disabled for thirty-eight years. The law did not help him, but when he met with Jesus, he was healed and his life transformed. The Pharisee's intention was to destabilise the miracles that took place. The same applies at this age, when trials come, nobody except Jesus. This man was set free and obtained the mercy of God, while Jesus ordered him to sin no more. Sinful acts are either inherited, through the family or personal behaviours that must have led to this unpleasant condition for so long. The focus is not to go back to the old pathway, nor dwell on the past that led him to sin, which is the devices of the devil that could lead to destruction.

The lame man of thirty-eight years struggled to be at the pool, awaiting the movement of water that seldom occurred for supernatural healing. If he did not come to the pool on that particular day, still awaiting anybody, he would have missed the miracles performed. May I submit that the best thing is for you to stand up, take action and do some work (noble deed) to provoke the blessing that will transform your life. We strive to live righteously according to the will of God, because a slothful creature cannot access the Kingdom alleyway.

Chapter Eight

PREPAREDNESS

The Bible stated that Heaven is specially prepared for those who are ready to do whatever it takes to enter through that narrow gate. Because God loves mankind, he deliberately made Heaven the ultimate target for all His creatures who are able to live in accordance with His will through holiness and righteousness, which is the only gateway to access. It was vividly stated in John 14:2-3:

2 *In my Father's house are many mansions: if it were not so, I would have told you. I go to prepare a place for you.*

3 And if I go and prepare a place for you, I will come again, and receive you unto myself; that where I am, there ye may be also.

So, Heaven is an abode for the redeemed, a resting place where the saved soul will live forever. It is where various activities are being executed, involving singing, praising, worshipping, reverencing God, and fellowshipping with Him routinely. The question is, how prepared are you for the second coming of Christ via this required pathway? There are signs that signify the coming of our Lord Jesus Christ as the disciples asked the Lord: but he responded in His words when you hear rumours of wars (Luke 21:7-24):

7 And they asked him, saying, Master, but when shall these things be? And what sign will there be when these things shall come to pass?

8 And he said, Take heed that ye be not deceived: for many shall come in my name, saying, I am Christ; and the time draweth near: go ye not therefore after them.

9 But when ye shall hear of wars and commotions, be not terrified: for these things must first come to pass; but the end is not by and by.

10 Then said he unto them, Nation shall rise against nations, and Kingdom against Kingdom:

11 And great earthquakes shall be in divers places, and famines, and pestilences' and fearful sights and great signs shall there be from Heaven.

12 But before all these, they shall lay their hands on you, and persecute you, delivering you up to the synagogues, and into prisons, being brought before kings, and rulers for my name's sake.

13 And it shall turn to you for a testimony.

14 Settle it therefore in your hearts, not to meditate before what ye shall answer:

15 For I will give you a mouth and wisdom, which all your adversaries shall not be able to gainsay nor resist.

16 And ye shall be betrayed both by parents, and brethren, and kinsfolk, and friends; and some of you shall they cause to be put to death.

17 And ye shall be hated of all men for my name's sake.

18 But there shall not a hair of your head perish.

19 In your patience possess ye your souls.

20 And when ye shall see Jerusalem compassed with armies, then know that the desolation thereof is nigh.

21 Then let them which are in Judea flee to the mountains; and let them which are in the midst of it depart out; and let not them that are in the countries enter there into.

22 For these be the days of vengeance, that all things which are written may be fulfilled.

23 But woe unto them that are with child, and to them that give suck, in those days! For there shall be great distress in the land, and wrath upon this people.

24 And they shall fall by the edge of the sword, and shall be led away captive into all nations: and Jerusalem shall be trodden down of the Gentiles; until the times of the Gentiles be fulfilled.

Therefore, saints of God, let us be sensitive, as demonstrated in these verses. Those are the signs of the end times. The whole world is undergoing various incidents that have never occurred before. The way forward is to be awake and adhere to the commandment and do in accordance to His will, for broad is the way that leads to destruction. There are rumours of war, pestilence and chronic illness despite medical research, confusion within the Governmental bodies, even nation rising against nation. All these are stressed by Christ as the end time signals, but be of good cheer, as you proclaimed Christ as your Lord and saviour, keep the lamp burning; victory is sure for eternal life. You and I shall not be as the unwise servants when the Master comes; He found them asleep.

We shall not be found wanting in Jesus' Name Amen.

According to Mark 13:32-37:

32 But of that day and that hour knoweth no man, no, not the angels which are in Heaven, neither the Son, but the Father.

33 Take ye heed, watch and pray: for ye know not when the time is.

34 For the Son of man is as a man taking a far journey, who left his house, and gave authority to his servants, and to every man his work, and commanded the porter to watch.

35 Watch ye therefore: for ye know not when the master of the house cometh, at even, or at midnight, or at the cock crowing, or in the morning:

36 Lest coming suddenly he find you sleeping.

37 And what I say unto you I say unto all, Watch.

The process to access this path might be very tough, as stated above, so we need to be wakeful and vigilant. It is for believers to realign appropriately and to be motivated in faithful living as a normal daily life because, as it was in the Old Covenant during Noah's era, so it is at this New Covenant period. Noah was instructed to build an ark, after prolonged warning, with a lot of persuasion. Noah made efforts to persuade people to change from their wrongdoings as it went beyond normality, but became an abomination that was extreme in the sight of God. As the people refused the awakening, subsequently the flood took over the earth. Thereafter, and regrettably, only the family of Noah were able to enter the ark, while the whole earth was destroyed.

Therefore, when there shall be a roll-call in the Heavenly Kingdom, we shall not be found wanting, in Jesus' name Amen. Nonetheless, In Genesis 7: 9-24:

9 There went in two and two unto Noah into the ark, the male and the female, as God had commanded Noah.

10 And it came to pass after seven days, that the waters of the flood were upon the earth.

11 In the six hundredth year of Noah's life, in the second month, the seventeenth day of the month, the same day were all the fountains of the great deep broken up, and the windows of Heaven were opened.

12 And the rain was upon the earth forty days and forty nights,

13 In the selfsame day entered Noah, and Shem, and Ham, and Japheth, the sons of Noah, and Noah's wife, and the three wives of his sons with them, into the ark;

14 They, and every beast after his kind, and all the cattle after their kind, and every creeping thing that creepeth upon the earth after his kind, and every fowl after his kind, every bird of every sort.

15 And they went in unto Noah into the ark, two and two of all flesh, wherein is the breath of life.

16 And they that went in, went in male and female of all flesh, as God had commanded him: and the LORD shut him in.

17 And the flood was forty days upon the earth; and the waters increased, and bare up the ark, and it was lift up above the earth.

18 And the waters prevailed, and were increased greatly upon the earth; and the ark went upon the face of the waters.

19 And the waters prevailed exceedingly upon the earth; and all the high hills, that were under the whole Heaven, were covered

20 Fifteen cubits upward did the waters prevail; and the mountains were covered.

21 And all flesh died that moved upon the earth, both of fowl, and of cattle, and of beast, and of every creeping thing that creepeth upon the earth, and every man:

22 All in whose nostrils was the breath of life, of all that was in the dry land, died.

23 And every living substance was destroyed which was upon the face of the ground, both man, and cattle, and the creeping things, and the fowl of the Heaven; and they were destroyed from the earth: and Noah only remained alive, and they that were with him in the ark.

24** **And the waters prevailed upon the earth a hundred and fifty days.

God is raising men and women of God globally towards the awareness of the Second Coming of our Lord Jesus Christ; thereby no one would perish. Despite a series of warnings, many perished according to the Old Testament from the above scripture, with years of prolonged warnings, alertness and awakening, to no profitable outcome; only Noah and his household were exempted from the disaster.

As Noah found grace in the eyes of the LORD (Gen. 6:8) both him and his household: May you obtain grace and the Covenant of Exemption by the Power in the Blood of Jesus, and it shall speak for you when and wherever needed in Jesus' Mighty Name Amen.

Consequently, the Lord is awakening His saints at this period, so that everyone is prepared, for churches and all nations to walk in the way of the Lord. Due to carelessness, unreadiness, slothfulness and lukewarmness without the ignition of the Holy Spirit was the life of the people during the era of Noah. The Lord is awakening His saints, these days not to be taken unawares, so that there shall be no loss of souls because of ignorance or disobedience. From the scenario of the ten virgins, while five were wise the other five were foolish. We shall not be foolish. The power of the Holy Spirit shall incubate our lives so that at the end we shall be accepted to reign with God in Jesus' Name Amen.

The account about the ten virgins was well analysed in Matthew 25:1-15:

1 Then shall the Kingdom of Heaven be likened unto ten virgins, which took their lamps, and went forth to meet the bridegroom.

2 And five of them were wise, and five were foolish.

3 They that were foolish took their lamps, and took no oil with them:

4 But the wise took oil in their vessels with their lamps.

5 While the bridegroom tarried, they all slumbered and slept.

6 And at midnight there was a cry made, Behold, the bridegroom cometh; go ye out to meet him.

7 Then all those virgins arose, and trimmed their lamps.

8 And the foolish said unto the wise, Give us of your oil; for our lamps are gone out.

9 But the wise answered, saying, Not so; lest there be not enough for us and you: but go ye rather to them that sell, and buy for yourselves.

10 And while they went to buy, the bridegroom came; and they that were ready went in with him to the marriage: and the door was shut.

11 Afterward came also the other virgins, saying, Lord, Lord, open to us.

12 But he answered and said, Verily I say unto you, I know you not.

13 Watch therefore, for ye know neither the day nor the hour wherein the Son of man cometh.

Jesus' means of preaching is routinely through ministering in the parables. He was expressing the scenario of the ten virgins for believers to be watchful for the second coming of Christ, as nobody knows the day, of His coming. The virgin signifies someone without blemish (living holy) thus: that reflected in your character, attitudes, your means of communication, your lifestyles are they in line with the Christian doctrine? Therefore, I implore you saints of God need to serve Him faithfully and fervently in readiness, just as five of the virgins were wise with enough oil, thus empowered by the power of the Holy Spirit in order to function as occasions demanded. No matter the circumstances, they were alert and prepared, persevered and were not weary nor lazy, while the other five were foolish, slothful, sluggish and lazy and by the time they went out to search for more oil, the bridegroom came and the door was shut against them. The foolish virgins, due to their unreadiness, procrastination and a nonchalant attitude, had chosen the broad way that led to destruction, while the wise virgins were honoured and accepted into the Kingdom of Heaven through the narrow way. Thus the way of holiness and righteousness entailed hard work, endurance, perseverance, prayerfulness, in preparedness and trusting Him by faith, because without Him we can do nothing.

Without doubt saints need to be on guide and able to be watchful. You should try to carry out self-examination if you wish to be in line with God's agenda. Are you a born-again Christian, or just being religious, or have you deviated from the narrow to the broad pathway? Noah's ark was shut, and only he and the members of his family were able to enter the Ark with the animals. Jesus is the way, the truth and the life.

The mercy of God shall not be shut against us, and the voice of condemnation shall not be raised against us in Jesus' Name. Amen.

Furthermore, the episode whereby Jesus went to the Mount of Olives whilst ministering to His disciples, who were asking about the signs of the end time. (Matthew 24: 3-15):

3   And as he sat upon the mount of Olives, the disciples came unto him privately, saying, Tell us, when shall these things be? and what shall be the sign of thy coming, and of the end of the world?

4 And Jesus answered and said unto them, Take heed that no man deceive you.

5 For many shall come in my name, saying, I am Christ; and shall deceive many.

6 And ye shall hear of wars and rumors of wars; see that ye be not troubled: for all these things must come to pass, but the end is not yet.

7 For nation shall rise against nation, and Kingdom against Kingdom: and there shall be famines, and pestilences, and earthquakes, in divers places.

8 All these are the beginning of sorrows.

9 Then shall they deliver you up to be afflicted, and shall kill you: and ye shall be hated of all nations for my name's sake.

10 And then shall many be offended, and shall betray one another, and shall hate one another.

11 And many false prophets shall rise, and shall deceive many.

12 And because iniquity shall abound, the love of many shall wax cold.

13 But he that shall endure unto the end, the same shall be saved.

14 And this gospel of the Kingdom shall be preached in all the world for a witness unto all nations, and then shall the end come.

15 When ye therefore shall see the ABOMINATION OF DESOLATION, spoken of by Daniel the prophet, stand in the holy place, (whoso readeth, let him understand).

This passage is the same as other gospels but much more detailed than the others, hence the crucial aspect is for believers to get prepared for His forthcoming, as Jesus declared that nobody knows the particular time, even Himself, except the Father. He gave the analysis of the signs in all the above verses; depicted all the negative happenings, which were nothing strange at this period, such as war, rumours of war, famine, pestilence, earthquakes, persecution, betrayal, hypocrisy, pride, materialism and profane teaching by some false prophets etc. Saints, be advised that we should endeavour to emulate and be ambassadors of Christ, and those called to minister should try as much as possible to avoid teachings that contradicts the Scriptures (heresy), not just to teach or preach what people want to hear. You and I cannot afford to please men and displease God, but must teach the undiluted Word of God (the gospel truth).

Many homes have been destabilised because of false men/women of God due to blasphemous teaching, heresy, hypocrisy or unrighteous living. We need to act as the good and faithful disciples of Christ to depopulate the Kingdom of darkness. The unbelievers are watching your character, your attitude towards your fellow men, either within your family, in the workplace or within the gathering of brethren, because, broad is that destructive pathway. You are implored to strive and walk in accordance with the precept of our Creator to gain access to His Kingdom.

Let's consider some of the teachings of Jesus. He always ministered in parables, like the one of the talents (Matthew 25:14-25):

14 For the Kingdom of Heaven is as a man travelling into a far country, who called his own servants, and delivered unto them his goods.

15 And unto one he gave five talents, to another two, and to another one; to every man according to his several abilities; and straightway took his journey.

16 Then he that had received the five talents went and traded with the same, and made them other five talents.

17 And likewise he that had received two, he also gained other two.

18 But he that had received one went and digged in the earth, and hid his lord's money.

19 After a long time the lord of those servants cometh, and reckoneth with them.

20 And so he that had received five talents came and brought other five talents, saying, Lord, thou deliveredst unto me five talents: behold, I have gained beside them five talents more.

21 His lord said unto him, Well done, thou good and faithful servant: thou hast been faithful over a few things, I will make thee ruler over many things: enter thou into the joy of thy lord.

22 He also that had received two talents came and said, Lord, thou deliveredst unto me two talents: behold, I have gained two other talents beside them.

23 His lord said unto him, Well done, good and faithful servant; thou hast been faithful over a few things, I will make thee ruler over many things: enter thou into the joy of thy lord.

24 Then he which had received the one talent came and said, Lord, I knew thee that thou art an hard man, reaping where thou hast not sown, and gathering where thou hast not strawed:

25 And I was afraid, and went and hid thy talent in the earth: lo, there thou hast that is thine.

You are destined to reign! It is your gifts that make room for you. The above emphasised the necessity for personal preparation and faithful service for the Master's use. The person with one talent was an unprofitable, slothful and unfaithful servant to his master. The concept is that many people out there are not contented with whatever position they occupy nor with what gifts or talent they possess. It reflects on their behaviour towards their leaders, either within the body of Christ or in the workplace. Immediately their Pastors, or their Manager or Director is absent, they pay lip service and are hypocritical and disloyal. They actively function when their leaders are present, but in their absence they never perform. Christ reproves this type of attitude, which is ungodly. It means that you are not a good follower of Christ. As you are disloyal to your Master, the same applies to your fellow brethren, or your colleagues at work; such an act is against the will of God. The Lord wants you to follow the Kingdom values in order to access the right entry towards eternal life.

The Lord knows you better than yourself, so He has given to an individual the gift and the ability to function accordingly. Due to self-interest or discontent, many have gone astray and indulged in atrocities within the body of Christ, their families, even within the secular set-up. The fivefold ministries are working towards the same goal of Kingdom mandate. It is applicable to all the elements created by God, like the moon, stars, sun; they all have important roles to play. You can only function appropriately in the area of your calling or of your assignment. Many photocopies are out there; the more you aim to be like A or B, you just need to get a clarification from God, as rightly stated by Christ, to direct your path, because He is the way, the truth and the life. The narrow way could be challenging and intimidating, but that is the requirement for the Kingdom standards in order to achieve that positive commendation at last.

Subsequently, what about your heart towards your fellowman/woman, having the heart of forgiveness? Definitely, offences will come; how you handle them is what matters and is vital. Offences are inevitable; they are a reality, because you are dealing with human nature born of sinful nature unto the world (Luke 17: 1-4):

1 Then said he unto the disciples, It is impossible but that offences will come: but woe unto him, through whom they come!

2 It were better for him that a millstone were hanged about his neck, and he cast into the sea, than that he should offend one of these little ones.

3 Take heed to yourselves: If thy brother trespass against thee, rebuke him; and if he repent, forgive him.

4 And if he trespass against thee seven times in a day, and seven times in a day turn again to thee, saying, I repent; thou shalt forgive him.

We need to make a plea from God to create a clean heart and to renew the right spirit within (Psalms 51:10-12). We pray from within our inner minds with the conviction for God to forgive every trace of iniquity and seek for rebirth. When you are regenerated, forgiveness will be made easy as you seek for divine grace to relate with everyone because it is mandatory as a Kingdom outlined.

Unforgiveness is deadly and cancerous. It could hinder prayers and delay a good outcome. Holiness and righteousness are the pathway towards the narrow way that leads to eternal life. Similarly, as stated in Matthew 6:12: ***And forgive us our debts, as we forgive our debtors.***

This verse is recommending that believers' own duty is to make a demand for forgiveness of sin from the Lord for prayers not to be hindered. Hence we have no option but to do likewise to our fellow human beings. Although there are instances that will provoke to be offended, the Bible declared that we should endeavour to be at peace with all men, because naturally we are dealing with human nature.

May the Lord hear us as we call and may the power of the Holy Ghost rekindle any heart that is not living in accordance with His tenets, in Jesus' name Amen.

Therefore, as believers, you are advised not to be distracted by things of this world nor materialist entanglement. Do not get me wrong: it is good to be wealthy, but remember to seek ye first the Kingdom of God and His righteousness, and other benefits to make life comfortable shall be added, because things of this world are temporal.

This parable has various perspectives depending on your interpretation and the ways being addressed. As Jesus was busy doing His Father's business (Luke 2:49):

And he said unto them, How is it that ye sought me? Wist ye not that I must be about my Father's business?

Jesus Christ was accountable to both His earthly parent and His Heavenly Father. He was not distracted, but focused and actively executing the instructions given to Him. For that reason, saints of God, please let's be vigilant and endeavour to emulate Christ. Do not relent efforts in doing good, but be a Kingdom builder, by sharing His words, giving to the poor, equipping the saints, supporting the work of God etc. As Apostle John was the forerunner of Jesus, the same is applicable to you and me, reflecting through your lifestyle, your communication, attitude, and other positive characteristics that can be recorded in your account as a good ambassador of Christ. Thus in thoughts, words and doings for the propagation of the gospel. Therefore, strive to spread the good news, win souls for His Kingdom, and as you engage in doing your Father's business, He is at work on your behalf.

Chapter Nine

THE WORD

In the book of John, he was the forerunner of Jesus. He announced and introduced Jesus Christ to the world. Somebody needs to reference you for any appointment. It is the normal procedure within the secular world, even the ministerial system. The medium could only be conveyed through the spoken or written word. The focus now is the word of God. Jesus is the Word Himself; that can transform lives as indicated in (John 1:1-18):

1 *In the beginning was the Word, and the Word was with God, and the Word was God.*

2 *The same was in the beginning with God*

3 *All things were made by him and without him was not anything made that was made.*

4 *In him was life; and the life was the light of men.*

5 *And the light shineth in darkness; and the darkness comprehended it not.*

6 *There was a man sent from God, whose name was John.*

7 *The same came for a witness, to bear witness of the Light that all men through him might believe.*

8 *He was not that Light, but was sent to bear witness of that Light.*

9 *That was the true Light, which lighteth every man that cometh into the world.*

10 *He was in the world, and the world was made by him, and the world knew him not.*

11 He came unto his own, and his own received him not.

12 But as many as received him, to them gave he power to become the sons of God, even to them that believe on his name:

13 Which were born, not of blood, nor of the will of the flesh, nor of the will of man, but of God.

14 And the Word was make flesh, and dwelt among us, (and we beheld his glory, the glory as of the only begotten of the Father,) full of grace and truth.

15 John bare witness of him, and cried, saying, This was he of whom I spake, He that cometh after me is preferred before me: for he was before me.

16 And of his fullness have all we received, and grace for grace.

17 For the law was given by Moses, but grace and truth came by Jesus Christ.

18 No man hath seen God at any time; the only begotten Son, which is in the bosom of the Father, he hath declared him.

John's demonstration of how the Word becomes flesh is thus: Jesus Christ Himself is the living Word who existed before the beginning of creation. He came in person to communicate a glorious message of hope, grace and truth to God's creatures. The intense expression of God through Jesus Christ (Himself) is the Word full of authority, power and might. It can address any situation as you believe and apply the right word whenever you can for intervention. As it was in the beginning from the Old Covenant, so it is now in the New Covenant perspectives, even for evermore. So, He manifests Himself routinely for miracle signs, and wonders as indicated in Hebrews 13:8:

Jesus Christ the same yesterday, and today, and for ever.

Nevertheless, (Genesis 1:1, 3) still in the demonstration of the power of the spoken words:

1 In the beginning God created the Heaven and the earth

3 And God said, Let there be light: and there was light.

From the beginning of creation, which was

accomplished by His word, each command consists of a word of declaration. God said a creative command, accordingly: Let there be, and a summary word, and it was so as indicated in the Scripture. Likewise, a descriptive word when Jesus defeated Satan with the Spoken Word. So we need to make a demand and declare with the authority of His expression "It is written" to address any issues or concerns.

God spoke into creation, in honourable responsiveness, and through human mediators in the written Word.

(Psalms 119:105) ***Thy word is lamp unto my feet, and a light unto my path***

The spoken word of God carries anointing to release power for the enhancement of any given assignment. Although the Word of God institutes the fact that hearing enables someone to believe, while believing make room for receiving. It is for believers to go out there and spread the good news of Christ, because we are the light to enlighten the unbelievers (Romans 10:14,15):

14 How then shall they call on him in whom they have not believed? And how shall they believe in him of whom they have not heard? And how shall they hear without a preacher?

15 And how shall they preach, except they be sent? As it is written, HOW BEAUTIFUL ARE THE FEET OF THEM THAT PREACH THE GOSPEL OF PEACE, AND BRING GLAD TIDINGS OF GOOD THINGS!

This is solely presenting the universal proclamation of the gospel. Apostle Paul presents the reason why a collective assertion is important: thus the call must be followed by faith, also, faith must be preceded by hearing. This signifies that knowledge is an indispensable tool to belief. Faith must have effective content, while hearing necessitates a preacher. Furthermore, preaching the word requires being sent by God, somebody needs to go out to say, to witness, testify to the goodness of God in his/her life. Your word is a tool that can impact lives, your own testimony is the first point of contact for reassurance towards soul winning, that: If God can do this for A, He is able to do likewise for B while salvation thereafter is from God Himself. It is for believers to play their parts while God does His bit to win souls unto His Kingdom. His role is solely to do the conviction towards the salvation of a soul worn. Moreover, according to Romans 10:17:

So then faith cometh by hearing, and hearing by the word of God.

For that reason, believers have to be prompt in preaching the Word constantly as to whether it is suitable or not. To be our routine lifestyles by so doing, in proclaiming His words; the Kingdom of Heaven will be engaged with awaiting rewards.

Additionally, in (1st Peter 1: 22-25):

22 Seeing ye have purified your souls in obeying the truth through the Spirit unto unfeigned love of the brethren, see that ye love one another with a pure heart fervently:

23 Being born again, not of corruptible seed, but of incorruptible, by the word of God, which liveth and abideth for ever.

23 FOR ALL FLESH IS AS GRASS, AND ALL THE GLORY OF MAN AS THE FLOWER OF GRASS. THE GRASS WITHERETH, AND THE FLOWER THEREOF FALLETH AWAY:

25 *BUT THE WORD OF THE LORD ENDURETH FOR EVER. And this is the word which by the gospel is preached unto you.*

This emphasises the love as earlier mentioned in this book, which was the greatest and last commandment ordained by Jesus Christ. Hence, to be born again is the illustration of how a newly-converted mind is being renewed by the power of the Holy Spirit through the Word of God. Also, the demonstrations of how Jesus Christ offers salvation to humanity through sacrificial offerings, redeeming souls of the entire world. As a result, our salvation depends on the human viewpoint, our readiness in acceptance of that offer through His word. Hebrews 4:12:

For the word of God is quick, and powerful, and sharper than any two-edged sword, piercing even to the dividing asunder of soul and spirit, and of the joints and marrow, and is a discerner of the thoughts and intents of the heart.

His word is meant to impact on individual lives, depending on your faith. As an indication of how you have passion and love towards the word of God, it can do wonders, depending on how you utilise it by your obedience and faith in God. It could be reflected through your lifestyle, our relationship with our fellow men, living in a holy and righteous way as it is written, because the Scripture cannot be broken, for narrow is that way to the Kingdom of Heaven.

Through His words, Jesus declared those that rejected Him (John 12:48):

He that rejecteth me, and receiveth not my words, hath one that judgeth him: the word that I have spoken, the same shall judge him in the last day.

If you obey God, you will keep His commandment, for He is the Living Word Himself. It is subsequently your level of obedience that God needs to consistently fight your battle as He subdues all satanic forces that are working against your destiny. Therefore, preaching the Good News of Christ to an unbeliever signifies you are boasting about whom you believe thus: evangelism

Chapter Ten

SOUL WINNING

Proverbs 11:30: ***The fruit of the righteous is a tree of life; and he that winneth souls is wise.***

Soul winning is of God, and it is compulsory to embark on this spiritual journey. This is the medium to advertise Christ as a believer. Many people are out there who have no knowledge of who Jesus is. They believe something which they don't even have the interpretation or the meaning, just because of their family background. Some just perceived that they were brought to Planet Earth by chance. They need awareness of the Creator of Heaven and earth, and that is why believers, those good followers of Christ referred to as Christians, have an important role to play for humanity in order to access the constricted road towards eternal life.

Jesus Christ commenced His ministry alone. He started drawing men unto Himself; Andrew was the disciple of John the Baptist, the one who converted his brother Peter, also known as Simon after his encounter with Christ in (John 1:41):

He first findeth his own brother Simon, and saith unto him, We have found the Messiah, which is being interpreted, the Christ.

Apostle Peter lately in the ministry was one of His Apostles who won thousands to Christ and in multiplication many souls were added to the Kingdom of God. Subsequently, Philip, having an encounter with Christ, drew Nathaniel, who later gained many souls. As a result, there was an increase within the body of Christ. Every one of His followers worked towards the expansion, in soul winning as kingdom builder. Hence, it is a command from God to draw men unto the knowledge of Christ; this is one of the principles to gain access to the narrow gate.

How can it happen? Unbelievers do watch

Christians within their community, families, workplace, anywhere. You and I portrayed our beliefs through our actions, in loving one another, showing kindness, communicating with respect, moderation in our dress code, a dignified and lifestyle pleasing unto God or holy living. Your Bible is vital, but your attitude, personality and character as an ambassador of Christ are what people are reading. Brethren, as specified, it is very wise and rewarding to be a soul winner. One soul won expresses how the angels rejoice in Heaven, and God is happy with soul winners. Saints of God, let us therefore awake and go out there to go fishing for Christ. One good seed will multiply. Andrew introduced Christ to Simon his brother, who later became the leader. We shall also be useful vessels for His Kingdom.

Dear brother and sisters, are you still shying away from your calling? That is your place; a place of divine appointment with God. Wherever and whatever you find yourself doing, please do it diligently. Whether within the secular or spiritual realm, you are employed by God. You were assigned to utilize your gift, anointing, talent, education or certificate to the glory of God. It is not only when you perceived, by standing on the pulpit, before you are referred to as a minister, neither it is then, that you acknowledged that God had appointed you. No! Whatever your role or position/designation, it is the Lord's doing. So do it appropriately. As you arise and obey His commandment, the Lord will hear you in Jesus' name.

Elijah was instructed to depart from Cherif and to relocate to Zarephath, where a widow had been prepared for him (1st kings 17:8-16):

8   And the word of the LORD came unto him, saying,

9   Arise, get thee to Zarephath, which belongeth to Zidon, and dwell there: behold, I have commanded a widow woman there to sustain thee.

10   So he arose and went to Zarephath. And when he came to the gate of the city, behold, the widow woman was there gathering of sticks: and he called to her, and said, Fetch me, I pray thee, a little water in a vessel, that I may drink.

11   And as she was going to fetch it, he called to her, and said, Bring me, I pray thee, a morsel of bread in thine hand.

12 And she said, As the LORD thy God liveth, I have not a cake, but a handful of meal in a barrel, and a little oil in a cruse: and, behold, I am gathering two sticks, that I may go in and dress it for me and my son, that we may eat it, and die.

13 And Elijah said unto her, Fear not; go and do as thou hast said: but make me thereof a little cake first, and bring it unto me, and after make for thee and for thy son.

14 For thus saith the LORD God of Israel, The barrel of meal shall not waste, neither shall the cruse of oil fail, until the day that the LORD sendeth rain upon the earth.

15 And she went and did according to the saying of Elijah: and she, and he, and her house, did eat many days.

16 And the barrel of meal wasted not, neither did the cruse of oil fail, according to the word of the LORD, which he spake by Elijah.

This situation is almost intertwined with the event of the Last Pamphlet via the process of soul winning. A young lad working for God was out of zeal and curiosity able to rescue an elderly lady who was about to commit suicide after all the sharing of leaflets/pamphlets on that particular Sunday, because it was routine for the father and this boy to go out on evangelism after the service. The father could not go with him, but this young man insisted and tried more persuasion to impress the father, but later went out by himself. After doing all he could for that day, he refused to go back home with the one left-over pamphlet. As led by the Spirit of God, he persistently knocked on a particular door, sensing there was somebody inside. He would not leave the door, but the person inside refused to open it, thinking that when the stranger got tired, he would depart. The boy refused to leave the door, determined to continue knocking, and at long last, surprisingly, an old woman distracted by the banging of this young evangelist was sent to this woman as an angel of deliverance. The next Sunday this woman came to the service, where she shared her testimony and everyone learned the essence of soul winning.

It is a personal race, and a personal relationship with God. The boy refused to give up at the door and kept on knocking until she opened it. What have you been asking God to do? The answer is: do not give up, keep on praying and praising, and keep on trusting Him, because He cares for you. Pray until something positive happens.

Let us deliberate on the widow's episode. The widow's last meal was all she had; for her it was eat and die. She never realised that God was working behind the scenes, while an angel was sent who would rescue her during the season of famine when all hope had been shattered and lost. She honoured God, and perceived that the prophet Elijah was a man of God. She would have missed her divine appointment if she had failed to give her last meal. She was a hospitable and loving woman, and knew how to extend love and kindness to her neighbour. She was tested and passed, and was sustained all through that season of famine. When genuine faith is tested it brings glory to the Almighty God.

This woman believed in God, which was why she was able to perceive that Elijah was a man of God. She agreed to give her drink, and the man made an extra demand for food. She never knew it was sent by God. She obtained favour from God. She was not the only widow in the land, but God screened and saw her heart, and besides, He did not want her to perish. He remembered and granted her petition, and she was able to pay her debt and became automatically blessed in her act of obedience. This was like a form of sacrificial offering; all that she had she gave. As God gave His only begotten Son, this poor widow showed love and was kind enough to obey the man of God. This was also the demonstration of the love of God for humanity when He released His Son for the salvation of our souls (John 3:16):

For God so loved the world, that he gave his only begotten Son, that whosoever believeth in him should not perish, but have everlasting life.

Despite her own need, she still trusted in the Lord. What is in your hand? The Lord has released that one thing, that gift or talent, for your fulfilment. It is for you to guide that gift jealously for God's manifestation. You are the Bible that people are reading.

Evangelism is a precious assignment in the agenda of the Kingdom of God. Reflect back, and consider if this young boy had refused to go out due to the cold weather on that fateful Sunday, as the father was unable to go with him; that woman would have died. May the Lord have mercy and grant us the grace to win the lost souls as we co-labour in His vineyard.

The Good Samaritan was able to act with passion caring for someone. He broke free from the captivity of all kinds, like that of tribalism, cultural allegiance, hatred, even selfishness, but rather to influence his neighbour whom he never knew (Luke 10:33-37). Jesus was able to break the barrier of cultural differences while He requested the woman at the well to offer Him a drink, because, in accordance with their culture they had nothing in common with the Samaritans. However, this woman became the first lady evangelist (John 4:7-23):

7 There cometh a woman of Samaria to draw water: Jesus saith unto her, Give me to drink.

8 (For his disciples were gone away unto the city to buy meat.)

9 Then saith the woman of Samaria unto him, How is it that thou, being a Jew, askest drink of me, which am a woman of Samaria? For the Jews have no dealing with the Samaritans.

10 Jesus answered and said unto her, If thou knewest the gift of God, and who it is that saith to thee, Give me to drink; thou wouldest have asked of him, and he would have given thee living water.

11 The woman saith unto him, Sir, thou hast nothing to draw with, and the well is deep: from whence then hast thou that living water?

12 Art thou greater than our father Jacob, which gave us the well, and drank thereof himself, and his children, and his cattle?

13 Jesus answered and said unto her, Whosoever drinketh of this water shall thirst again:

14 But whosoever drinketh of the water that I shall give him shall never thirst; but the water that I shall give him shalt be in him a well of water springing up into everlasting life.

15 *The woman saith unto him, Sir, give me this water, that I thirst not, neither come hither to draw*

16 *Jesus saith unto her, Go, call thy husband, and come hither.*

17 *The woman answered and said, I have no husband. Jesus said unto her, Thou hast well said, I have no husband.*

18 *For thou hast had five husbands; and he whom thou now hast is not thy husband: in that saidst thou truly.*

19 *The woman saith unto him Sir, I perceive that thou art a prophet.*

20 *Our fathers worshiped in this mountain; and ye say, that in Jerusalem is the place where men ought to worship.*

21 *Jesus saith unto her, Woman, believe me, the hour cometh, when ye shall neither in this mountain, nor yet at Jerusalem, worship the Father.*

22 Ye worship ye know not what; we know what we worship for salvation is of the Jews.

23 But the hour cometh, and now is, when the true worshipers shall worship the Father in spirit and in truth; for the Father seeketh such to worship him.

Protocol was broken and cultural differences were disregarded. The Samaritan people had been despised by the Jews since the Old Testament period, for various reasons and because of their intermarriages with the gentiles among them. Hence, Jesus' teaching was in relation to the parable of the Good Samaritan, also of the ten lepers who were able to come back in an attitude of thankfulness, and there was gratification from the Samaritans. They were able to come back and honour God with hearts of appreciation. Jesus was demonstrating an act of passion, love and gratefulness to humanity. He is the living water. When you accept Him you will never lack any good thing. It does not matter about your family background, for God is no respecter of any person. He is a universal God, creator of the Universe. Your lifestyle can easily win souls for Christ; it is for you to have faith and believe in Him, abide to His commandment, which is the principle devices towards the Kingdom of Heaven via the narrow entry.

Can your neighbours perceive that you portray the emblem of Christ? Are you still nailing Christ to the cross for a second time? Would your way of life enable you to preach the gospel of Christ without shame? The Bible declared that you are the light of the world. So, brethren, consider your ways and if you are still in doubt, or making any decision of following Christ, I rather suggest to determine and make the effort to let your light shine in the midst of darkness, because you are on a mission (Matthew 5:16):

Let your light so shine before men, that they may see your good works, and glorify your Father which is in Heaven.

So, beloved saints of God, endeavour to be concerned about Heavenly riches. Be a good role model and a "shining light" in every dimension: be a good ambassador for Christ. As you lay up your treasures in Heaven by generously contributing towards God's work at any given opportunity, such as giving to the less privileged, working for God in your local assembly, living a life that pleases God, do His will as you obey the commandment, love to one another, as mentioned on this manuscript according to the Scriptures. Believers are the light of the world. Hence, we possess the light of the day. We must work not to conquer, acquire, or to accumulate and retire, but to make it known to the whole world as we propagate the invisible Christ by touching people with the love of Christ. Then we have the confidence that our labour is not in vain. Jesus has laid down for us an example; we have no choice but to emulate him in exercising love and doing works for His Kingdom in humility. It is good to invest, but always remember that you will leave all behind at the end of the day.

You are implored to make an effort to routinely carry out self-assessment, and consider your ways, as you and I do the evaluation, to see if they are in line with the Kingdom standards as you make Heavenly riches your main focus. Thus, lay up your treasure in Heaven where there is no depreciation. Moreover, God has given the body of Christ to tread via the constricted pathway through His grace and mercy before it is too late for reconciliation. I suggest that if any area of your life is not with God's word, it is time for repentance and to be transformed. Please be aware that heaven and hell are real. The choice is for the individual to tread through the accepted pathway to reign and rule with Christ in the Heavenly Kingdom, where there will be no more pain nor sorrow but gloriously worshipping God. Therefore, endeavour to work out your salvation with fear and trembling. If you have not yet surrender your life to Christ, it is time to do so. For narrow is that way towards the Kingdom of Heaven, that shall be our lot, in Jesus' name amen.

CONCLUSION

Satan was cast out because of pride, thinking he was the only one in charge. May we not be cast away in the Kingdom of Heaven as we strive to stride through the narrow path. That is to avoid or deviate from what God has proven in His word that He hates, specifically those deadly sins as recorded in the Book of Proverbs 6:16-19. These are the roots of disobedience, right from the beginning of the human race. They are a key for believers to keep His laid down principles in obedience. In all you get, the important thing is to achieve wisdom, which is the principal thing inculcated in love. For Jesus is love. Hence love towards one another, and not being hypocritical, because God sees your heart. Therefore, believers must make every effort to be righteous, to have the right standing with God. It is not the law written in stone, but on every individual heart that is vital. The law may direct you how to conduct yourself, but the Spirit of God demands that you have a personal relationship with God. That could have an impact on your attitude, character, things of God and your dealings with other fellow men. As children of God, we should try as hard as possible to guide against a sinful way of life. If you realise you have fallen into any sin, you must automatically confess your sin to Jesus, the great intercessor, in order to restore your fellowship back to the Father. For God's love to mankind, He gave His only begotten Son as a gift of life. Also endeavour to live a righteous lifestyle, as without holiness no one can please God. For that reason, if you say you love God whom through faith you believe in Him; but do not extend love towards your neighbour; that means the person has no love or compassion and is unable to care for fellow human beings as the Good Samaritan did. Additionally, from the account of Abraham and the Shunamite woman:

Abraham and the Shunamite woman, with their wealth, were able to show kindness. and little did they realise that they were able to entertain angels of God because they were sensitive to things of the spirit, and a fear of the Lord. While this woman was blessed with a child, a promise from God came into manifestation due to their obedience to the will of God. If any of them were proud, they would not have been able to show kindness nor entertained strangers. It added value to their family.

Conversely, whatever position or status you have, always remember that it is not by your power, nor by might, but by the Spirit of the Living God that you are able to attain that position. He owns the key to success and without Him you and I cannot achieve, but be encouraged to abide in Him and lived a holy and righteous lifestyle for His Kingdom.

Also, a lying tongue will be involved with the shedding of innocent blood, evil plotting and running negative errands that can easily lead to mischief within the community or gathering of saints. With negative pronouncements, sowing the seeds of discord, many brethren have backslidden due to bad attitudes and ungodly behaviour within the Church. Vatshi was displaced due to disobedience to her husband, and high look that was unacceptable behaviour, while Esther was replaced. People with proud eyes will definitely never communicate nor relate with someone who is not of high social class or reputation. God hates this, so I suggest you should avoid becoming the object of His wrath.

With all the above, an individual can by His grace gain access to the Heavenly Kingdom via the strait gate. Jesus Christ is a precious sacrificial offering of salvation for humanity. Negative characteristics cannot gain access via the constricted way. For that reason, the Lord made a demand that we all make the effort to live a life that pleases God, which will give us access to life eternal through the narrow gate. Therefore, you are a treasured vessel of God. May you attain a great reward as you tread via the straitened entry toward eternal life in Jesus' name Amen.